E-Business and ERP

Transforming the Enterprise

Grant Norris
James R. Hurley
Kenneth M. Hartley
John R. Dunleavy
John D. Balls

JOHN WILEY & SONS, INC.

New York • Chichester • Weinheim • Brisbane • Singapore • Toronto

This book is printed on acid-free paper. ∞

Published by John Wiley & Sons, Inc.

Published simultaneously in Canada.

This publication is designed to provide accurate and authoritative
information in regard to the subject matter covered. It is sold with the
understanding that the publisher is not engaged in rendering legal,
accounting, or other professional services. If legal advice or other expert
assistance is required, the services of a competent professional person
should be sought.

Designations used by companies to distinguish their products are often
claimed as trademarks. In all instances where John Wiley & Sons, Inc. is
aware of a claim, the product names appear in initial capital or all capital
letters. Readers, however, should contact the appropriate companies for
more complete information regarding trademarks and registration.

Library of Congress Cataloging-in-Publication Data:

E-business and ERP : transforming the enterprise/Grant Norris ... [et al.].
    p. cm.
   Includes index.
   ISBN 0-471-39208-1 (cloth : alk. paper)
    1. Production management. 2. Management information systems.
  3. Business planning. 4. Electronic commerce. I. Norris, Grant.

TS155.E67 2000
658.4'038'8011—dc21   00-039231

Printed in the United States of America.

10 9 8 7 6 5 4

About the Authors

Grant Norris, B.S., M.B.A, is a partner in PricewaterhouseCoopers' management consulting services practice. Mr. Norris has 17 years of experience designing and installing ERP and e-business systems for a variety of organizations in the telecommunications, transportation, defense, and energy industries. He has lectured on topics related to this experience at a number of software conferences and at the St. Joseph's University Business School. Mr. Norris's global perspective results from his having lived and worked in Canada, Europe, the Middle East, and the United States. He is co-author of *SAP: An Executive's Comprehensive Guide.* E-mail: grant.norris@us.pwcglobal.com.

James R. Hurley, B.A., M.B.A., CAGS, CPA, a partner in PricewaterhouseCoopers' management consulting services practice, is that organization's North American SAP practice leader for the telecommunications industry. Mr. Hurley specializes in ERP and e-business in the finance, telecommunications, and manufacturing industries. Co-author of *SAP: An Executive's Comprehensive Guide,* he has, for the past 15 years, worked at some of the world's largest consulting organizations, helping clients to apply technology to their businesses. E-mail: james.r.hurley@us.pwcglobal.com.

About the Authors

Kenneth M. Hartley, B.S., M.B.A., CFPIM, is a Pricewaterhouse-Coopers partner with more than 15 years of experience helping a variety of major international companies in such areas as process improvement, supply chain management, and manufacturing systems design and implementation. His articles have appeared in several professional industry journals in the United States and abroad. E-mail: kenneth.m.hartley@us.pwcglobal.com.

John R. Dunleavy, B.A., M.B.A., CPA, is a partner at PricewaterhouseCoopers and the global leader of its e-business initiative for the financial and cost management practice. He has developed performance measurement and management reporting hierarchies for a number of major telecommunications companies. Mr. Dunleavy has also consulted with international telephone companies on the privatizing and restructuring of their financial systems. Co-author of three books—*Reinventing the CFO, SAP: An Executive's Comprehensive Guide,* and *Shared Services: Adding Value to the Business Units*—he has lectured at the Amos Tuck and Columbia Graduate Schools of Business. E-mail: jack.dunleavy@us.pwcglobal.com.

John D. Balls, B.A., M.S., M.B.A., is CIO, Vice President, and Program Director for a leading Fortune 100 communications company's enterprise resource planning (ERP) initiative. He has extensive experience in operations, marketing, sales, product management, strategic planning, organization design, information technology, business management, and financial management. A 29-year communications industry veteran, Mr. Balls has held numerous senior leadership positions in these areas and has led several business process reengineering and organizational transformation initiatives. Additionally, he has been a guest speaker, contributor, and active participant at a number of business process re-engineering conferences and forums. E-mail: johndballs@yahoo.com.

Foreword

Those focused on technology view the merger of Time Warner and America Online as a remarkable event. This largest transaction of its kind in history married an Internet company to a traditional media company, technology to content, e-speed to business speed. While this deal clearly demonstrates the real value of the Internet and e-business, it also marks the start of the "click-and-brick" era, confirming what many have long suspected: Traditional companies must embrace the Internet to survive, but, at the same time, pure Internet companies benefit from the assets and infrastructure of their "bricks-and-mortar" counterparts.

The blending of Internet technologies and traditional business concerns is impacting all industries and is really the latest phase in the ongoing evolution of business. Take the automotive industry, for example. Since pioneering the division-of-labor approach to manufacturing, the automotive industry has led in embracing innovative approaches by reengineering business processes; implementing materials requirement planning (MRP), manufacturing resource planning (MRP II), and just-in-time (JIT) manufacturing; and installing enterprise resource planning (ERP) software. Today, the Internet is driving the current industry goals of achieving a five-day order-to-delivery cycle, global reach, and personalization. It is behind decisions to outsource manufacturing. It is redefining the role of dealers and their relationship with the consumer and renewing the role of the brand owner. In short, the Internet will do for the automotive business today what the introduction of the assembly line did for the industry a century ago. However, without connecting order delivery, manufacturing, financial, human resources, and other back-office systems to the Internet, even companies with long track records of innovation are not likely to succeed.

These challenges are not limited to the automotive industry. They affect all companies, both virtual and traditional. On the one hand, Internet companies, despite the megahype to the contrary, must still establish and execute efficient business processes to make and move product, market and sell, manage finances and employees, and grapple with regulatory bodies. On the other hand, traditional companies will have to respond to the strategic opportunities arising from the Internet and e-technology or face extinction.

All companies, however, will need to update their business infrastructures and change the way they work to respond more immediately to customer needs. The Internet, with its ability to connect customers and suppliers at e-speed, is certainly a critical component of this change. Web portals will play a major role, but they are not the whole answer. The existing internal infrastructures of today's global enterprises represent a huge investment in technology, learning, and business engineering research that has been going on, in some cases, for hundreds of years. In the last 15 years, this investment has contributed to the greatest productivity gains achieved since the computer was invented some 50 years ago.

The most successful companies will be those that leverage this investment by implementing e-business solutions supported by sound existing infrastructures based on well-functioning ERP systems. Rather than discarding past gains, today's executives should be asking themselves: How do we get the most out of our investments in current infrastructure? How do we penetrate the Internet marketplace with current assets? How do we compete against pure dot.com companies?

The authors of this book propose that the answers lie in a combination of speed, business capability, technical know-how, and, perhaps most important, execution. Their message is that companies best positioned to succeed at e-business are those that have solid business infrastructures utilizing ERP-based software and capabilities. This comprehensive book:

- Presents a framework for understanding e-business opportunities within the context of a traditional enterprise and its infrastructure.
- Demonstrates why companies need e-business technologies that tightly link the information capabilities of their customers, suppliers, and other business partners with their existing ERP systems and information stores.
- Explores the idea that while the Internet drives new business strategies, ERP is a necessary component in making them work.
- Reviews models for valuing technology and other infrastructure investments.
- Analyzes how the Internet impacts supply-chain management, customer relationship management, and shared services.

The authors also explore how the cultures of an enterprise and its business partners can impact success. And, perhaps most important, they utilize a newly developed ERP e-business matrix to demonstrate how an enterprise can migrate from its current position in the ERP/e-business panorama to the position it desires to occupy in the future—a migration that must and will include e-business as a core competency but that also relies heavily on a well-implemented and -maintained ERP-based infrastructure or backbone.

Managers at all levels will benefit from reading this book. It provides answers to complex questions and pragmatic, straightforward advice on moving any enterprise forward at this crucial time, when success will depend on balancing existing strengths with new capabilities to capitalize on the tremendous opportunities that lie ahead.

Ric Andersen
Partner, PricewaterhouseCoopers LLP

Acknowledgments

Writing this book would not have been possible without the help and dedication of numerous individuals whose contributions to this project made the sometimes arduous journey from concept to publication much easier. We thank them all for their invaluable assistance.

We especially thank Ric Andersen for his unwavering support. Ric inspired us, contributed to our ideas, guided us, and encouraged us to work on this project.

Gene Zasadinski edited our manuscript with a dedication and attention to detail that will benefit every reader. More than anything, we appreciate the style and tact Gene brought to the task of providing us much needed input. Thank you, Gene.

Without Jon Zonderman this book would not have been written. Jon contributed to our ideas, helped us understand our own thoughts more clearly, and kept us focused on the work at hand. We owe Jon many thanks for his central role in this project.

We would like to thank Yolanda White for producing every figure in this book. Her creativity and technical skills transformed our "scribbles" into the high-quality graphics that so greatly enhance the text.

We are most grateful to those colleagues who reviewed our manuscript: Ryan Balsam, Chris Bennett, Ed Berryman, Jeff Brugos,

Acknowledgments

William Dauphinais, William Q. Davis, Martin Deise, David Duray, Volker Flottau, Robert Freeman, Felix Giebfried, Larry Hupka, Mark E. Johnson, Lawrence Kenny, Joel A. Kurtzman, John Leffler, Bruce A. Levy, Roger Lipsey, Cathy Neuman, Edward M. Pillard, David A. Pleasance, Roderick N. Roy, William Serrao, and Peggy Vaughan. They spent many hours of personal time contributing to and refining our ideas, and, perhaps most important, challenging our words. We sincerely appreciate their effort.

Andrew Alpern and Edward Silver provided us with legal advice and constructive feedback on our manuscript. Sheck Cho and members of his editorial and design team at John Wiley & Sons worked tirelessly on our behalf. We thank each of them for their support.

Cynthia A. Angle, Charlene Ardent, Lori A. Bagent, Lorraine M. Buck, Jacqueline Collette, Maureen A. Connolly, Beth Dunleavy, Antonio Hernandez, Monica O'Shaughnessy, Eileen Peat, Kimberly Wood, and Connie Yee-Cohen helped administer this project. We thank them for their patience with our unachievable deadlines and for all of their good work.

Finally, we thank our family and friends who gave up so much to enable us to complete this project. Without their tolerance and understanding, this book would not exist.

Grant Norris
James R. Hurley
Kenneth M. Hartley
John R. Dunleavy
John D. Balls

Contents

Contents

Contents

Contents

Introduction

For decades, management theorists have believed that companies could and should forge tighter links up and down the supply chain, from raw materials to customers. Since the late 1990s, companies have increasingly turned to Internet- and Web-based technologies to accomplish this. But what they are finding is that without enterprise resource planning (ERP) software, sharing accurate information with their trading partners is impossible.

What we are coming to realize through our work with clients is that properly implementing e-business and ERP technologies in harmony truly creates a situation where one plus one equals more than two. Web-based technology puts life and breath into ERP technology that is large, technologically cumbersome, and does not always easily reveal its value. At the same time, ERP allows e-business to come into full flower, putting real substance behind that flashy Web page. While ERP organizes information within the enterprise, e-business disseminates that information far and wide. In short, ERP and e-business technologies supercharge each other.

ERP AND E-BUSINESS: AN EVOLVING RELATIONSHIP

ERP is the latest in a number of manufacturing and financial information systems that have been devised since the late 1940s to streamline the information flow that parallels the physical flow of goods, from raw materials to finished products. This flow of information occurs within an enterprise as well as between the enterprise and other entities (providers of services to the company) immediately up and down the supply chain and end users.

From the 1950s to the 1980s, much work went into streamlining the flow of materials. However, the information-centric aspects of business, such as order taking and order fulfillment, were suboptimized or defeated by interconnectivity/communication issues. Even today, many companies find it difficult to move reliable information quickly across the supply chain. For example, something as simple as stock levels and availability may not be accessible in a timely manner to all parts of an enterprise, let alone to dependent business partners.

The first steps in systematizing information flow around the manufacturing process were taken as early as the 1960s when materials requirement planning (MRP) software became available. In the 1980s, efforts were made to make these applications more robust and better able to generate information based on a more realistic set of assumptions. These efforts resulted in manufacturing resource planning (MRP II) software. Finally, in the 1990s, software developers created ERP software, a fuller "suite" of applications capable of linking all internal transactions.

In the past couple of years, e-business has exploded on the scene, and some advocates claim that it is the ultimate solution to this information management problem. While traditional production-management information systems (MRP, MRP II, and ERP) have focused on the movement of information within an enterprise, Web-based technology facilitates movement of information from business to business and from business to consumer, as well as from consumer to business.

The days when the Internet was primarily a research tool are long gone. Today, it is positioned as the engine that will drive the future of business. Research groups such as Forrester, Gartner, and AMR all project incredible growth for e-business in the first five years of the new century. According to analysts, now that companies are mostly finished upgrading their information technology to accommodate both the new millennium and the Euro, they are truly free to put their resources into revolutionizing their business models through e-business.

Some argue that in their rush to become an e-business, most companies will decide against implementing an ERP system, stop a current ERP development in its tracks, or even backtrack away from ERP as the technology of transaction processing because of the compatibility issues involved in making third-party e-business applications work fluidly with any of the current suites offered by ERP providers. What we are finding, however, is that some client companies are building e-business applications and largely ignoring ERP development, hoping someone, someday will integrate the back end. As a result, companies whose e-business applications have no order-fulfillment and order-status capabilities either lack data or need to recreate it.

Some advocates of e-business claim that Web-based technology can effectively supplant internal information systems, especially for information companies that do not actually make or transport a physical product. The most aggressive of these even claim that Web-based technologies do the same in manufacturing companies.

The electronic enterprise, they argue, is a company that has in place Web-based electronic communication with all of its partners on both the supply and demand sides. Transaction processing inside the enterprise, they claim, can be carried out via the software of these front-end communication systems and passed from one to the next. We believe, however, that an internal enterprise transaction engine, independent of the supplier- and customer-facing front ends, is necessary for any company large enough to be considered an enterprise. To date, the best of these internal transaction engines are driven by ERP software. The issue, then, is far more complex than the e-business evangelists make it out to be. E-business simply does not work without clean internal processes and data.

The choice, though, is not between developing e-business solutions or implementing ERP. Clearly, both are necessary. In the future, ERP will integrate and evolve with a host of other technologies that cumulatively support the e-business model. In fact, this is already happening. But for today and for the purpose of discussion, it is still necessary to distinguish the transaction processing function of ERP from the communications capabilities of e-nabling technologies. The question is when to put resources into which technology in order to maximize the effectiveness of both over the long term.

ERP/E-BUSINESS CHALLENGE: SHEDDING OLD NOTIONS

Making ERP work most effectively in an e-business environment means shedding old notions of ERP. One such notion is that ERP will always look the same. ERP software in the next few years will certainly not look like ERP software designed in the 1990s. The delivery of ERP functionality will also change.

For instance, a software vendor that today focuses on one front-end e-business application may in the future build into its products a transaction engine component that can then be attached to other companies' front ends. Or a company may design an internal transaction engine that can only process transactions from one e-business front end to another. (This might be called the "ERP light" or "mini ERP" scenario.) The other option: ERP vendors will successfully make products more flexible and less difficult to implement; and they will either add e-business functionality or make their systems more compatible with third-party front-end e-business products.

Why is this a challenge for ERP vendors? Companies use ERP software to enable processes that confer a competitive edge (for example, pricing, promotions, special configurations, or bundling of products and services). These complex and often unique processes do not often operate well out in the open over the Internet.

E-business is forcing ERP vendors to rethink their products' role within the enterprise. All, in one way or another, are looking to broaden ERP functionality to incorporate front-end technology, to create trading communities through portals, and to joint venture with

Web-based technology and other vendors. At the same time, third-party vendors are chipping away at ERP's stranglehold on internal enterprise functionality.

For instance, SAP has introduced mySAP.com™. PeopleSoft is introducing a 100 percent iClient version. Oracle has completely reengineered its ERP products to be Internet technology and has dropped client-server architecture. Microsoft is busily defining application protocol interfaces (APIs) for Windows 2000. i2, a provider of supply-chain-management software, is attacking ERP vendors from that flank. RosettaNet is setting standards for data exchange. Extricity is positioning its product to be the Internet communications middleman, and Neon wants to help link the Internet to existing enterprise applications. Commerce One and Ariba are positioned to connect buyers and sellers on the Web.

Another notion that must give way is that an ERP system necessarily will sit physically in the enterprise's facility or be managed by the enterprise. In the future, ERP management may be outsourced even more than it is today, freeing many companies from the burdens of installation and maintenance. For many companies, ERP itself may be delivered over the Web through business application outsourcing undertaken by application service providers (ASPs).

In outsourcing, the service provider operates the ERP in a way mutually agreed on with the client. The client holds the license to the software but does not have to undertake the effort and resource expense to operationalize it. Software is held on the outsourcing service provider's server and customized to the client's need. Some ERP vendors are looking to provide software in this way, as are providers of other applications and third parties who are willing to run any number of different applications. An ASP relationship, sometimes called "hosted" or rented applications, delivers the application one way, take it or leave it. It is up to the client company to redesign its business processes to align them with the application being delivered.

Today, the ASP approach is especially suitable in a company for which basic transaction processing is not a core competency. In the future, a company's ability to convert transactional data into business knowledge and intelligence in order to support decision making will be key to its success. Also in the future, enterprises will determine the cheapest way to generate reliable, complete, and consistent transactional data. So far in computing history, this has been an expensive process.

NEW TECHNOLOGIES, NEW OPTIONS

Today, most companies are focusing their e-business efforts on simple e-buy and e-sell applications. The dominant philosophy is "build it and they will come." But for most traditional businesses—o–r "non-dot.com companies," as they are coming to be known—Web-based selling is cannibalizing their other sales channels.

Pure dot.com companies are stealing some market share from non-dot.coms, but some dot.coms are finding that as they grow exponentially, their internal transaction processing systems are not robust enough to handle the volume of sales. Some non-dot.coms have also found that when business begins flowing through their Web-based sales channels, their internal systems are not up to the task.

Today, the market for new technologies is robust. Many start-up companies are producing niche-focused products for e-selling or for supply-chain management, for example. ERP vendors are also reacting, working to build the same functionality into their product suites. Two of the early niche players in these areas—Siebel in customer relationship management (CRM) software and i2 in supply-chain management (SCM) software—are quite large and are squeezing ERP vendors from outside the enterprise.

The purpose of these new technologies is to e-nable the extended value chain. In the future, it is clear that companies will work together in extended value chains. Those that are able to plug their internal information systems into the information chain that parallels the physical-goods value chain will prosper; those that are not will fail. Successful companies will be part of a networked team of business partners dedicated to delivering customer value. Very few (if any) companies will be able to compete single-handedly against such a team. The technology to "team" is available today, and strong teams are already beginning to form.

In short, together, e-business technologies (the Internet, the Web, a host of e-nabling technologies) and ERP will provide companies with new options for raising profitability and creating substantial competitive advantage. In the remainder of this book, we explore a number of those options and their implications for companies competing in an e-business environment. We also examine the role of ERP today and in the context of new business models that are enabled by e-business and associated technologies and that represent the next step in organizational evolution—a step with potentially revolutionary impact.

1

Concepts Behind the Electronic Enterprise

In the few short years since it first appeared, Web-based technology has already had an enormous impact on consumers and businesses around the world. Other technologies, including enterprise resource planning (ERP) in the 1990s, have been important phenomena. But e-business has been a revolution. As Figure 1-1 illustrates, while it took 16 years for the number of personal computer (PC) users to grow to 50 million, Internet users grew to the same number in only four years, once the technology became available to the public.

ADAPTIVE VERSUS DISRUPTIVE TECHNOLOGY

While ERP is an adaptive technology, e-business is a disruptive technology. Adaptive technologies move earlier technologies forward incrementally. Disruptive technologies change the way people live their lives or the way businesses operate. For instance, while the touch-tone telephone was an adaptive technology, the telephone itself was disruptive; while the electric train was an adaptive technology, the train itself was disruptive.

As Figure 1-2 illustrates, the life cycle of most technologies begins with initial hype, and is followed by learning and experimenting, a sec-

Figure 1-1   Comparative Adoption Time to 50 Million Users

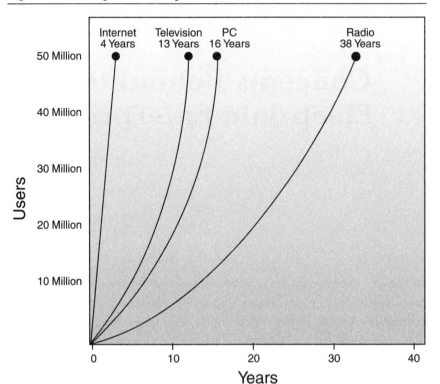

ond wave of technology, and a consolidation of the infrastructure. Only then do they achieve critical mass. As the dotted lines indicate, the life cycle of disruptive technologies, such as the Internet and e-business, goes from initial hype to critical mass in the blink of an eye.

Figure 1-3 illustrates the life cycle of a disruptive technology, in this case steel-producing minimills. Clayton M. Christensen of Harvard Business School uses this well-known example in his book, *The Innovator's Dilemma.*

Throughout the 1970s, major steel companies declined to get into the minimill business because, at the time, those facilities produced only low-quality steel that competed with their commodity rebar operations. However, by the 1980s, minimill steel quality was

Figure 1-2   Life Cycle of Adaptive versus Disruptive Technologies

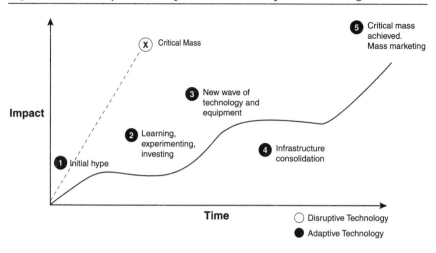

vastly improved, and the minimills' competitive pricing took vast amounts of business from traditional open-hearth mills.

A similar situation is occurring with e-business. In the business-to-consumer (B2C) arena, many bricks-and-mortar companies did

Figure 1-3   Life Cycle of a Disruptive Technology

not recognize the true competitive advantage that dot.com companies had in reaching retail customers until they lost large portions of their market share. In the business-to-business (B2B) arena, companies that do not recognize the power of e-business will shortly find themselves locked out of participation in the most aggressive value networks.

E-business is disruptive because it changes the basic way in which businesses interact with business partners and customers. It focuses on relations outside the company's four walls and, in theory at least, will force the company to live up to outsiders' expectations.

ERP, however, was an adaptation and refinement of earlier data processing technologies. It merged finance, procurement, and manufacturing planning and refined the logic of those earlier technologies. It was a huge jump, mostly because it forced companies to align business processes with information processing logic.

Although e-business is rapidly changing the basic paradigm under which businesses operate, a company is able to fully realize the opportunities of e-business only if it has strong, integrated internal information systems, that is, one of the ERP systems, working together with a third-party software developer (for example, SAP working with SpaceNet as a front end).

DEFINITIONS OF ERP AND E-BUSINESS

It is important to define clearly what we mean by ERP and what we mean by e-business.

ERP

ERP is a structured approach to optimizing a company's internal value chain. The software, if fully installed across an entire enterprise, connects the components of the enterprise through a logical transmission and sharing of common data with an integrated ERP. When data such as a sale becomes available at one point in the business, it courses its way through the software, which automatically calculates the effects of the transaction on other areas, such as manufacturing, inventory, procurement, invoicing, and booking the actual sale to the financial ledger.

What ERP really does is organize, codify, and standardize an enterprise's business processes and data. The software transforms transactional data into useful information and collates the data so that it can be analyzed. In this way, all of the collected transactional data becomes information that companies can use to support business decisions.

ERP software is not intrinsically strategic; rather, it is an enabling technology, a set of integrated software modules that make up the core engine of internal transaction processing. Implementing ERP requires major changes to organizational, cultural, and business processes. Many of the ERP products developed in the 1990s caused companies to redesign their business processes to eliminate non–value-adding work, freeing employees to focus on truly value-adding activities, dramatically increasing a company's productive capacity. Among the key drivers of process redesign is the need to improve the company's financial performance by improving operational performance. Long-term financial gains can occur only when a company delivers increasing customer value while simultaneously lowering the cost of delivering that value.

All too often, ERP software was—and still is—seen purely as a means of cutting costs. As a result, organizational resistance to ERP implementation has often been strong, and not all ERP implementation programs delivered the promised enterprise improvements. We now know that the key to change is the willingness of individuals throughout the enterprise to adopt not only new technology but new ways of working. In an ERP-empowered organization, new technology and processes force individuals to upgrade their skill set.

The implementation of ERP software and the business process change that must simultaneously occur necessarily affects a business's organizational structure and, more importantly, the individual roles within the organization. Many process redesign efforts and software implementations lead to staff reductions. In growing companies, people can be moved into other areas. In flat or declining companies, the change management needed to carry out a successful process change or system implementation is more complex. These issues also appear in e-business implementations, and any lessons learned from a previous ERP implementation can be useful in that regard. One thing we do know is that changing skills is a very important factor in ERP implementation. It may be even more important in the e-business world.

E-Business

Electronic business encompasses three stages: e-commerce, e-business, and e-partnering. The early stages of a company's e-business activity are almost always focused on reaching the customer, the later stages on streamlining value-chain activities to deliver more value to the customer.

E-commerce either leverages an Internet-based sales channel to enhance marketing and sell products or services, or leverages the Internet to make purchasing more efficient. E-commerce allows these purchases and sales transactions to occur with minimal disruption to organizational culture and business processes.

E-commerce includes the e-storefront and e-catalog, e-billing and e-payment, and rudimentary forms of e-procurement. Electronic data interchange (EDI) is one technology that has enabled B2B e-commerce for many years; today's Web-based technologies do away with the necessity for EDI, a unique, dedicated, and custom technology shared by two companies. Unfortunately, many companies still need EDI to communicate with legacy systems. However, because of the ubiquity of public Internet technology since the mid-1990s, nearly every company today must have the capacity to do business over the Internet.

E-business improves business performance by using electronic information technologies and open standards to connect suppliers and customers at all steps along the value chain. E-business can significantly improve business performance by strengthening the linkages in the value chain between businesses, and between a business and the ultimate consumer. Whereas e-commerce focuses on efficiency in selling, marketing, and purchasing, e-business focuses on effectiveness through improved customer service, reduced costs, and streamlined business processes. For some companies, e-commerce will be the core of their electronic business strategy; for others, it will be a part of a more comprehensive e-business strategy.

Streamlining business processes in the e-business world involves two imperatives: trust among business partners and agreement on standard ways of working, and agreement on a common data language that facilitates dialogue on mutual business events over the Internet.

An extreme view is that a virtual company manages only product development, marketing, pricing, manufacturing, cash collections, and accounting. Third parties do the rest. E-business applications manage supplier data, customer data, and all associated transactions. The company puts together a sell plan and a build plan, and that's it. Figure 1-4 illustrates one possible strategy for a virtual company and its value chain.

Figure 1-4   A Possible Value-Chain Strategy for a Virtual Company

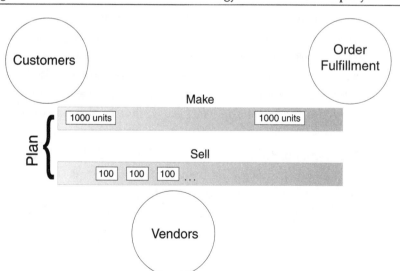

E-partnering is an intense relationship between businesses that utilize e-business capabilities to create an environment for shared business improvements, mutual benefits, and joint rewards. More than simply linking business systems, e-partnering is a strategic, customer-focused relationship in which companies work together to optimize an overall value chain.

BASIC ASSUMPTIONS

In discussing the relationship between e-business and ERP technologies, the following assumptions underpin our point of view.

- **Assumption 1:** Except for a very few companies that do nothing but aggregate information and match buyers and sellers, all companies need some sort of internal transaction engine to match the internal information flow with the actual flow of goods and/or services, as well as money. For the most part, every company has certain business information tasks it must perform. These are facilitated by ERP. Web-based technology comprises the "electronic" portion of the electronic enterprise, but ERP comprises the "enterprise" portion.
- **Assumption 2:** E-business is best supported by a well-tuned ERP system (ERP in its broadest definition). Although the e-business front end (Web site) garners the most attention today, especially from consumers, what lies behind the Web page (ERP) is far more important. ERP is necessary to fulfill the promises made on the Web page, that is, the promise of e-business.
- **Assumption 3:** No one path will lead to success. Each company needs to decide its own strategy, in terms of both ERP implementation and e-business. That strategy will be driven by customer demands, competitive pressure, and the current state of the enterprise—its willingness to change as well as its technical capabilities—and the state of the enterprise's business partners and their systems.

ERP/E-BUSINESS MATRIX

Figure 1-5 illustrates a new e-business model developed by PricewaterhouseCoopers.[1]

In order to make rational decisions about how to deploy resources in implementing either e-business, ERP, or both, a company must know both its starting position in the e-business panorama and its desired end state, relative to the various possibilities. To facilitate this, we have designed an e-business/ERP matrix (Figure 1-6). This matrix has on its horizontal the five possible places on an e-business landscape, and on its vertical, five possible places on an ERP landscape.

Figure 1-5　E-Business Panorama

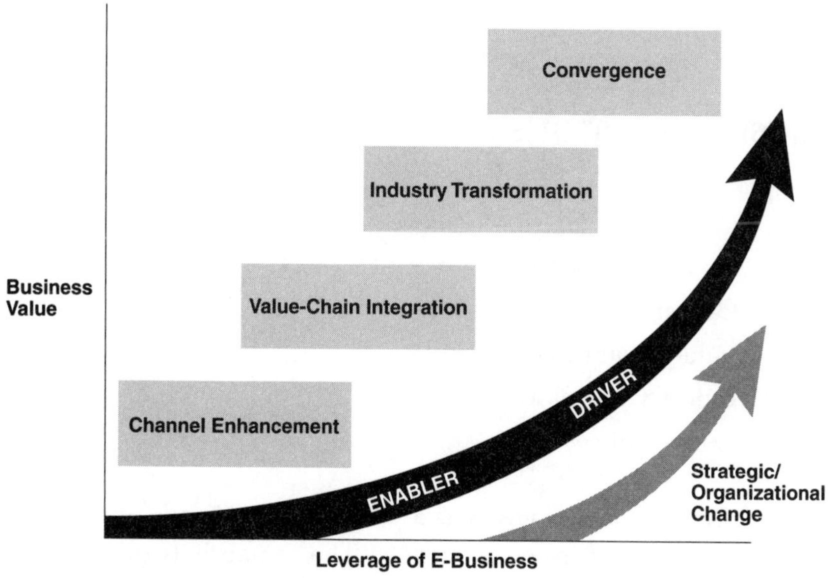

[1] For a detailed discussion of this model, see Martin V. Deise, Conrad Nowikow, Patrick King, and Amy Wright, *Executive's Guide to E-Business: From Tactics to Strategy* (New York: John Wiley & Sons, 2000).

Figure 1-6   ERP/E-Business Matrix

	No E-Business Capabilities	Channel Enhancement	Value-Chain Integration	Industry Transformation	Convergence
Greenfield					
Nonintegrated Systems					
Limited/Single-Function ERP					
Integrated Business-Unit ERP					
Integrated Enterprise ERP					

E-BUSINESS OPTIONS

The five options on the e-business matrix are:

1. No E-Business Capabilities[2]
2. Channel Enhancement
3. Value-Chain Integration
4. Industry Transformation
5. Convergence

E-business can be viewed as a panoramic landscape, made up of a series of snapshots from left to right. These snapshots overlap each

---

[2] In our matrix, we have added "no e-business" as a starting point to the four-snapshot model to accommodate start-ups that have no capabilities in either e-business or in ERP. This "blank slate" starting point is necessary for our discussion of migration-path options in Chapters 9 and 10.

other; in this way the edges are not lost, but the boundaries are also indistinct. Not all portions of a company—especially a multi–business-unit company—need to occupy the same snapshot at the same time. It is important to note that as a company moves across the e-business panorama, e-business becomes more of a driver of the company's business model. Also, from left to right, the amount of strategic and organizational change increases in each of the panorama's four snapshots.

No E-Business Capabilities

Although there are fewer every day, some companies still have not attempted e-business. But given the rate of growth in the e-business environment, remaining in the no e-business stage is not a valid alternative.

Channel Enhancement

Most companies enter e-business with point solutions such as selling over the Web, providing customer self-service, and conducting Web-based indirect procurement. Within this space, companies use Web technology as an enabler. They modify existing business processes and in some cases create new processes targeted at improving business performance. In so doing, they are engaging in e-commerce—the marketing, selling, or buying of products and services over the Internet.

Value-Chain Integration

As companies master channel enhancement, most explore opportunities to use e-business to integrate customers' and suppliers' operations with their processes and systems. In this space, companies strive to use the Internet to implement e-customer relationship management (eCRM) and e-supply chain management (eSCM) capabilities. These allow companies to link their operations seamlessly with those of customers and suppliers. On the customer side, companies are creating personalized Web sites and portals to simplify transacting business over the Internet and to capture customer information. On the supply side, companies are sharing design, planning, and forecasting information with suppliers to increase the velocity of bidirectional information flow. Since the Internet provides a low-cost medium for the movement of information, many companies are once again considering outsourcing as a process efficiency alternative.

Industry Transformation

Industry leaders push the envelope of e-business capabilities to transform their strategies, organizations, processes, and systems to achieve competitive advantage. Since the industrial revolution, businesses have used the same basic model to compete in the marketplace. But e-business is creating ways for companies to maximize shareholder value by completely transforming their industries. Companies that want to create an industry-transformation business model are aligning their strategies with their core competencies and using the Internet as a tool to offload non-core parts of their businesses. These companies are also establishing strategies to counteract the movement of intermediaries into their selling chain, driving a wedge between them and their customers. Additionally, they are examining the opportunity to use the Internet to integrate service offerings into their customer's businesses and to operate the non-core parts of their businesses. The line between companies becomes less pronounced as they and their partners link internal systems through the Web, creating new markets, new opportunities, new customers, and new products and services.

Convergence

Industry convergence is the coming together of companies from different industries to provide goods and services to consumers. Convergence is not solely a function of e-business or Internet technology; it is equally a function of industry deregulation, globalization of business, evolving customer demand, and new competitive tactics. The Internet enables these companies to easily partner in developing products and services geared toward providing customers a one-stop shop. In theory, convergence could occur without e-business. However, as the cost of moving information continuously declines, industry convergence becomes easier and cheaper to accomplish. E-business positions an enterprise to pursue convergence as a business strategy because of both the decreasing costs and the rapid adoption of technology.

ERP OPTIONS

We have defined the five possible ERP spaces for a company as greenfield, nonintegrated systems, limited-single-function ERP, integrated business unit ERP, or integrated enterprise ERP. In reality, a single enterprise may not map perfectly to any one of these spaces. However, these categories provide a framework for discussing available options in a meaningful and understandable manner.

Greenfield

A greenfield company is a new company with no history of information systems. Such a company can create an information system architecture from scratch. Without any legacy systems or ERP, such a company is free to develop a path to its desired state of e-business and to let its e-business progress drive its selection of an internal transaction engine.

Nonintegrated Systems

By definition, a company with nonintegrated information systems has no rapid and meaningful data exchange between its internal systems that record business events. It may have a different type of engine for each business unit or corporate function. Such a company relies heavily on "black box" software and manual processes to work data throughout the enterprise. Software maintenance and development costs are high, and the enterprise probably does not adapt readily to change.

ERP by Function

A company with ERP by function has successfully installed one or a few major ERP modules (most often the finance, human resources, and/or manufacturing modules) across all of its business units. Probably, such a company has undertaken this work in the context of cost cutting and still remains suboptimized across the enterprise. Internal value chains at these companies are likely to require manual intervention and management.

ERP by Business Unit

A company with ERP by business unit has successfully installed a fully integrated ERP suite in one or more business units, thereby increasing its ability to handle the volume of customer and supplier transactions that come through the e-business front-end systems.

Ideally, such a company operates as a "holding company," presiding over the unrelated value chains of the various business units. Suppliers, customers, products, and management are not linked in any way, and synergies among business units do not exist. Also, where ERP is implemented by country, there is little or no integration of data across national borders.

Fully Integrated ERP

Very few companies fall into this category, in which a fully integrated ERP suite has been implemented across the enterprise. Companies in this category have a distinct advantage: They have the internal transaction engine in place to deliver on the promises of the company's Web pages, and the ability to truly show "one face to the customer," not only in front-end Web-page design, but also in the way Web-based functions integrate with internal "back-office" functions.

For customers, this integration means that Web-based entry flows directly into real-time available-to-promise and order fulfillment. For suppliers, it means that the company truly is able to manage the flow of materials into the production process to the advantage of both parties rather than merely to push inventory onto the supplier.

DOMINANT ARCHITECTURE IN THE ERP/E-BUSINESS MARRIAGE

As ERP and e-business technologies compete for dominance in the future, companies constructing their systems architectures can choose between two main options: a more fully integrated ERP system that adds robust customer relationship management (CRM) and supply-chain management (SCM) modules, as well as Web-based interfaces with outside entities; or a best-in-breed portfolio-assembly model.

A multivendor solution gives a company the opportunity to purchase the best in class of each functional module. However, implementing this solution may mean increased costs and a need for greater resources. A single-vendor, packaged solution may ease the implementation but may also sacrifice functionality and features available in any particular area. Many vendors of ERP and e-business solutions are using Internet portals to combine both options. Through a single portal, a user can enter a universe of integrated solutions to myriad problems.

In the consumer world, portals began as research tools, similar to search engines, that scoured the databases of member organizations rather than searched the entire universe of the Internet. Users are able to create a personalized view of the Web, utilizing a variety of tools and information sources, to obtain only vetted information. Portals also act as places to hatch communities and dynamically exchange information using many different media (direct messaging, Internet protocol [IP] telephony, video, message posting, etc.).

In the B2B universe, a portal is coming to mean an association of vendor companies that utilize the portal to deliver to potential purchasers a host of solutions to related problems. The tools available in today's portals are becoming more powerful all the time. The line between portals and application service providers is already indistinct.

2

Inside Out, Outside In: Complementary Technologies of ERP and E-Business

In the world of twenty-first-century business, ERP and Internet technologies are rapidly coming together. However, today that merging is incomplete and its exact nature is unclear; therefore, it is important today for companies embracing an e-business model to understand each technology and its functionality separately.

ERP is the internal technological hub of a single enterprise. Web-based technology extends each enterprise's internal information infrastructure into the external environment, representing the company brand and projecting it to the marketplace. ERP is focused on internal process efficiency and effectiveness. E-business is focused on external, cross-enterprise process efficiency and effectiveness and on product promotion. While ERP technology supports current business strategy, e-business opens the door to new strategic opportunities. To marry ERP and Web-based technology successfully and push each to achieve its maximum benefit, the providers of each must understand the benefits that each provides to the other.

Today's ERP systems, when fully installed as integrated suites, can be thought of as central repositories of internal corporate information derived from five major processes: finance, logistics, manufacturing, human resources, and sales and marketing. As illustrated in Figure 2-1, ERP software helps organizations effectively and efficiently manage all their internal information resources to meet overall goals.

As illustrated in Figure 2-2, Web-based technology provides connections via the Internet to a host of external parties. Stand-alone e-business software is available for each of these relationships, usually from providers who focus on building the best application to handle any given process. Software has also been developed to help manage

Figure 2-1   ERP Focuses on Internal Enterprise Data, Information, and Knowledge

Figure 2-2   E-Business Focuses on Communication with External
                    Stakeholders

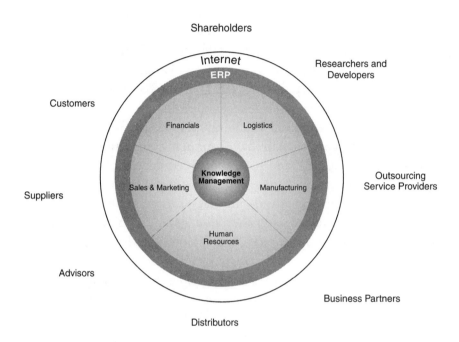

many of these relationships. In Figures 2-1 and 2-2, knowledge management is not associated with any one technology. Rather, it is depicted as a process that requires an organization to tap the data in all information channels and consolidate that information so that it is meaningful to the business.

MAKING THEM WORK TOGETHER

E-business applications look inward from outside the enterprise, seeking to connect an outside entity with the enterprise's information. At the same time, ERP, which has traditionally been focused solely on internal activities, is being forced to look outward from the inside, seeking to provide enterprise information to all of the various outside partners.

Some argue that because Web-based technologies are disruptive, they will supplant all others. But we believe that is not the case. ERP will always have value. As an adaptive technology, it supplants previous generations of technology that focused on the same problems, most notably materials requirement planning (MRP) and manufacturing resource planning (MRP II). Web-based technology, by contrast, attacks a totally different set of problems.

Viewing the issue from a different perspective, others argue that e-business applications will have enough transaction processing power to supplant ERP and have the added benefit of being able to "hand off" transactions to other e-business applications. For instance, a Web-based order-entry front end that customers can use will hand off the transaction to an application that generates material orders to the front end that suppliers use, and the one that logistics providers use, and so on.

To be sure, this technical feat is possible, at least in theory. However, achieving it poses two major problems:

1. Even if one envisions many of today's large producers of physical goods as future information-only companies, somewhere, at the end of the chain of information, things have to be made. The entity with internal processes that have to do with physical production needs an ERP or comparable enterprise-wide transaction processor to keep track of money, people, raw material, work-in-process, and finished-goods inventory. The now-famous shipping and returns problems experienced during the 1998 and 1999 holiday shopping seasons is ample evidence of this.

2. Once any organization grows to a certain size—even one such as financial services, which produces no true physical product—it must consolidate financial and human resources information in such a way that ERP becomes appropriate. In some cases, processes can be outsourced to third-party

providers, as long as they are not core or strategic to the enterprise. But a company cannot outsource all of its business processes. No company will ever be so virtual that it does not need to manage people and money and to remain compliant with the regulatory environments within which it operates around the globe.

There is also a practical rather than philosophical difficulty with Internet-based technology trying to supplant ERP technology. While ERP functionality may be delivered by Internet-based technology in the future, the functionality will still be that of ERP. Oracle is already moving in this direction. If providers of Web-based technology endeavor to solve the problems ERP already addresses, they may, in fact, pull their resources away from enhancing their pure Web-based technologies and possibly suffer the consequences.

First, such a play would be a disservice to customers who are looking for cutting-edge Web-based technology. It may also put companies at a competitive disadvantage against those that continue to focus on pure e-business solutions. The better approach for e-business solution providers may be to seek to build their products so they offer the easiest integration with current and next-generation ERP technology.

Second, the business and process knowledge built into existing ERP packages is very deep, and ERP software is mature and proven. Recreating it as a Web-based technology means rewriting, retesting, and, perhaps most importantly, retraining employees on unproven application software—hardly an efficient undertaking.

Providers of these technologies ultimately will see themselves not as competitors, but as providers of complementary products and services. This view is reinforced by the large and growing portfolio of "middleware" that can be used to integrate ERP and Web-based technology. The best middleware is completely neutral—the Switzerland of software—and allows any ERP vendor's products to connect with various e-business applications.

ERP: THE HUB OF A SINGLE ENTERPRISE

An integrated ERP system is the hub of an enterprise and is used to support existing business strategies. ERP provides a company the flexibility required to improve customer responsiveness (the demand side) and to better manage production needs and inventory (the supply side). It is also the ultimate tool for effective allocation of a business's scarce resources. With ERP, a company can create a new information foundation by replacing many legacy systems of varying vintages that house data in different ways. Senior management can use ERP to gain control over information and improve decision support. ERP also provides a consistency of information across a global enterprise and integrates the following:

- ○ Resource planning, which includes forecasting and planning, purchasing and material management, warehouse and distribution management, product distribution, and accounting and finance. By providing timely, accurate, and complete data about these areas, ERP software helps a company to assess, report on, and deploy its resources quickly and to focus on organizational priorities. For example, a company can assess its total cash position globally for a large supplier who may also be a customer. All too often, bills are paid to suppliers who are also customers and who owe more than they are owed.

- ○ Supply-chain management, which includes understanding demand and capacity, and scheduling capacity to meet demand. By linking disparate parts of an enterprise with ERP, more efficient schedules can be established that satisfy, in an optimal way, the enterprise's needs. This reduces cycle time and inventory levels, and improves a company's cash position.

- ○ Demand chain management, which includes handling product configuration; quotes, pricing, and contracts; promotions; and commissions. By consolidating information with ERP, contracts can be better negotiated; pricing can be established to consider the total enterprise-wide position; and sales offices can be better assessed, rewarded, and managed.

o Knowledge management, which includes creating a data warehouse, a central repository for the enterprise's data; performing business analysis on this data; providing decision support for enterprise leadership; and creating future customer-based strategies. These activities comprise a management information system (MIS), which facilitates the making of appropriate business decisions. In this capacity, ERP evolves from a transaction-processing engine into a true distiller of information. Data warehousing can become a powerful tool for corporate executives and managers only if it is fed with data that is consistent, reliable, and timely.

In a fully integrated ERP system, these activities are accomplished by utilizing five tightly integrated modules: finance, manufacturing, logistics, sales and marketing, and human resources.

Finance

When compared to legacy systems, ERP software significantly reduces the cost of financial record keeping. As corporations grow through acquisition, and as business units are allowed to make more of their own decisions, some companies create forests of competing and sometimes conflicting financial management data and software.

The consistency of ERP system data provides improved information for analysis and a seamless reconciliation from the general ledger to subledgers. The data is updated in real time throughout the month, and a basis for linking operational results and the financial effects of those results. With ERP, a physical transaction cannot be booked without the resulting financial effect being shown. This visibility of activities across finance and operations allows operational managers to better understand the effects of their decisions. The company's financial organization is better equipped to provide decision support to corporate leadership, to create strategic performance measures, and to engage in strategic cost management.

31

Manufacturing

With ERP software's ability to explicitly link the operational and financial systems, an enterprise can easily show how operational causes equal financial effects. The software provides a consistent set of product names in a central product registry; a consistent way of looking at customers and vendors; integration of sales and production information; and a way to calculate availability of product for sales, distribution, and materials management.

An integrated ERP system also enables better order-to-production planning by linking sales and distribution to materials management, production planning, and financials in real time; real-time visibility of customer orders and customer demand; and modeling of anticipated orders. With ERP, sales opportunities turn into orders based on past performance information; stock can be adjusted nearly instantly; and detailed manufacturing resource planning can be performed daily.

Logistics

ERP integrates distribution more tightly with manufacturing, sales, and financial reporting, thereby enhancing reporting of future performance indicators as well as past performance measures. The software provides an integrated basis for managing the signals that support the distribution environment necessary to meet twenty-first century customer desires and demands. ERP technology supports strategic purchasing and "materials only" costing rather than standard costing. Aligned performance indicators, rather than traditional indicators that measure functional silos, support customer-driven, low-cost operations. ERP also supports cross-functional, process-driven, customer-focused logistics and distribution.

Sales and Marketing

ERP software enhances an enterprise's sales efforts in a number of ways. Performing profitability analyses requires real-time data for costs, revenue, and sales volumes. With ERP, the company can perform profitability analysis, showing profits and contribution margins by market segment.

With ERP software, it is also possible to design sophisticated pricing procedures that include numerous prices, discounts, rebates, and tax considerations. Any pricing element can be maintained by any number of specific criteria, including any combination of customer, customer group, material, material group, and sales channel.

Finally, sales organizations can use ERP to project much more accurate delivery dates for orders. In an e-business environment, customers will be able to receive over the Web much more accurate delivery date information, and, when ERP is properly linked to an e-business front end, look into the company's finished-goods and work-in-process inventories, as well as materials availability to determine how quickly an order can be filled.

Human Resources

ERP supports an enterprise in its human resource planning, development, and compensation areas. It provides an integrated database of personnel (employed or contracted), maintains salary and benefits structures, supports planning and recruiting, and keeps track of reimbursable travel and living expenses. ERP does payroll accounting for a wide variety of individual national requirements and allows a company to centralize or decentralize the payroll function by country or by legal entity.

ERP records individual qualifications and requirements used for resource planning; enhances career and succession planning, and coordination of training programs; and maximizes time management, from planning to recording and controlling time, including shift planning, time exception reporting, and time reporting for cost allocation where staff charge their time to specific cost objects such as projects or service orders.

ERP ALONE FALLS SHORT OF TWENTY-FIRST CENTURY CUSTOMER DEMANDS

Despite all of its virtues, ERP by itself falls short of meeting today's customers' demands for better service. These customers want speed and self-service in their transactions, including the ability to do their own product configurations, and more integration of product and service.

Customers, whether retail consumers or distributors and suppliers, also want lower costs and higher quality, both in the product and the service, and they want their entire relationship with the enterprise to be highly personalized. At a minimum, this means having detailed order information on hand, and should include at least an element of personalization, such as the status of other orders, offers of related products, and personalized screens that make the transaction easier for the individual, with fewer clicks and faster paths in. For example, etoys.com allows a user to create a wish list of items, costs, personal annotations, and totals. The wish list can then be saved, turned into an order, or e-mailed to someone else, who can then turn it into an order.

Meeting these demands is a tall order that cannot be filled by ERP alone. Why? Companies are being driven to higher levels of efficiency and effectiveness. They are being forced to innovate at an ever more rapid pace. They are looking to business-process outsourcing to run the processes they find they cannot make more efficient and effective. They are finding that they must work more closely with business partners to meet customer demands. Very few companies will be able to go it alone in the new marketplace that is emerging. Strategic partnerships based on trust and respect must be forged with capable and reliable companies committed to changing the way they do business at all levels and willing to share risks and profits appropriately. Internal processes are being forced to become more tightly aligned to customer demands. Sales and service are converging and are being forced to deliver a higher level of reliability. Supply chains are being driven to become more efficient. Currently available ERP suites simply were not designed to accomplish these goals.

E-BUSINESS PROVIDES THE IDEAL EXTENSION TO INTERNAL PROCESSES

Web-based technology moves information through value chains, bringing together previously separate groups who can communicate faster and more efficiently via telephone, fax, or e-mail than they could face to face. Web-based technology has the capacity to provide information instantaneously at a low cost.

Customer Focus

Today, customers expect more than ever before. To meet these expectations, products are becoming products and services. Companies are becoming "me businesses," providing accessibility when, where, and how customers want it. Customer expectations now include individualized service, low-cost products, short cycle times, and accurate delivery dates.

With the availability of Internet-based research services, customers have more price information than ever before. They know not only the price of the product, but also the price of the service and the cost of the transaction. They know what they are getting and what they are paying for it. For example, 800.com and many other Web sites will do a price and feature comparison on-line in seconds that previously took days or even weeks of research to accomplish. Armed with this information, customers are making ever more challenging demands and are often two clicks away from finding another supplier. This increased information available to customers is a critical issue for many managers.

Companies are being forced to redesign their traditional processes of sales, service, and marketing by trying to redefine the customer relationship within a comprehensive, integrated customer relationship management (CRM) process. They are producing customer-centric applications and using information to try to get ahead of the competition through highly effective business relationships and value-added services.

New technology is allowing companies to collect information on their customers' buying habits and patterns and to use it in future interactions. This approach, which is individual and unique to each customer–supplier relationship, cements long-term relationships, benefits the customer, and creates loyalty and trust.

Interactive Relationships with Value-Chain Partners

Companies derive much competitive advantage today from their ability to relay information quickly through the value chain. The ability of each participant to retrieve information from a tightly integrated value chain and then to act on it results in greater value for customers.

A company that combines ERP technology with Web-based technology looks something like Figure 2-3. In addition to the e-buy and e-sell front ends, front ends are also available for e-human resource self-service (sometimes referred to as e-associate), e-collaborative planning, and e-logistics. With the e-buy/ERP/e-sell enterprises extended across the value chain, companies can create tightly linked extended enterprises, which we call *extraprises*. The big question for ERP vendors, e-business front-end technology vendors, and enterprises alike is: What will that model look like when fully formed? There are three alternatives (see Figures 2-4, 2-5, and 2-6).

Figure 2-3   ERP and Web-Based Technology Together Extend the Enterprise

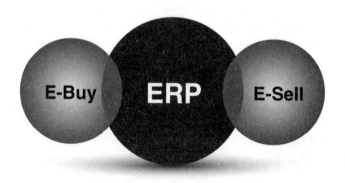

Figure 2-4   Extended Value Chain with Third-Party Portals

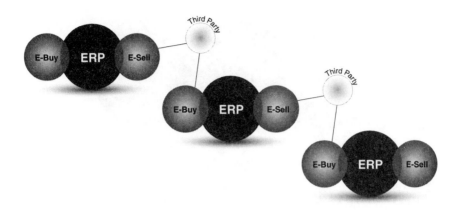

Figure 2-4 is a model of an extended enterprise in which parties connect with each other through third parties—aggregators of buyers and/or sellers—who create and manage marketplaces. These marketplaces may be collated catalogs, such as those provided for maintenance, repair, and operations (MRO) materials by such companies as Ariba. They may also be industry marketplaces that can be set up as an auction, a bid-and-ask market, or a third-party matchmaker. Alternatively, they could be portals or even "workplaces," like that being created by SAP under the name mySAP.com.

In Figure 2-5, the value chain is connected company to company, with each company's e-sell channel connecting directly to the

Figure 2-5   Extended Value Chain: Buy-Side Front End Connects to
            Sell-Side Front End

Figure 2-6   Extended Value Chain: ERP to ERP Connections

e-buy channel of the next company upstream in the production process. In this model, common part numbers are necessary, not only from each company's e-buy and e-sell to its internal ERP system, but also from each company's e-buy to other companies' e-sells and from each company's e-sell to other companies' e-buys. Industry standards are important here, especially in heavily regulated industries. Increased use of Extensible Markup Language (XML)–a data exchange standard complementary to Hypertext Markup Language (HTML)–and standards organizations like RosettaNet and the Organization for the Advancement of Structured Information Standards (OASIS) facilitate this approach. The ability to achieve this kind of integration increases if each party uses the same transaction system, such as SAP or Oracle.

In Figure 2-6, each company's ERP system connects directly to the ERP systems of suppliers and customers. Electronic data interchange (EDI) offers a similar model, although in the EDI model each enterprise must create unique protocols for each supplier or customer. In an Internet-based model with open standards, a company could connect through Web-based technology with each supplier and each customer.

Because information is more easily available using Web-based technology to connect to both suppliers and customers, the opportunity exists for an enterprise to create new business strategies based on transforming a value chain into an integrated value network. The reason for this relates to the unique attributes of information:

○ Information can be consumed multiple times.
○ It is hard to determine information's value prior to making a purchase.
○ Information can be condensed.
○ Information's value changes with time and usage.
○ Information opens doors.

In such a universe, each enterprise can be an information hub. The key to being an information hub is owning the customer interface. The customer interface is both where the enterprise—or the hub of an integrated value network—provides value to the customer and where it provides value to the network by gathering customer data that can then be transformed into usable information and knowledge about customer needs and desires.

The more enterprises are connected to the network, the more value there is for any one enterprise in being connected to this extended enterprise. Ever-increasing customer value drives more entrants to the network. As the network partners learn to work together better, the customer benefit increases as costs decrease and service levels improve. Success breeds success.

This dynamic—network economies of scale—becomes a virtuous circle, driving members of the extended enterprise to constantly improve their own internal processes as well as the cross-enterprise network processes. Network members strive for cost effectiveness, reduction, and avoidance. In this environment, a company that produces a finished good can have relationships with a number of suppliers of intermediate-step products. Using information technology, a company can create a product flow chain that best suits its needs at that time. The product flow chain consists of providers who are best able to deliver particular assemblies, or simply through the providers who have the capacity at the time the order is entered.

Figure 2-7   Traditional and E-Business Value Chains

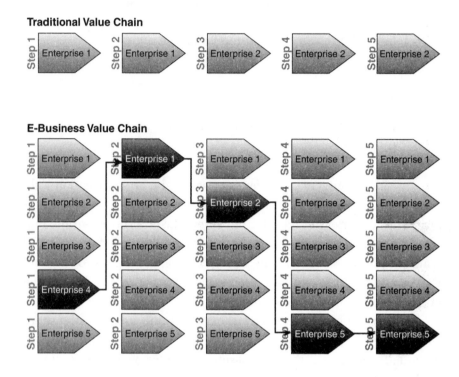

This dynamic is illustrated in Figure 2-7, which shows both the traditional value chain and the potentially dynamic e-business value chain. Such global connectivity and communication speed demands that each member of the network become increasingly flexible and open. Openness, trust, flexibility, and access to the information network—the Internet—are prerequisites to being able to make intelligent choices.

ERP Boosts E-Business Potential

Communicating with partners in the supply chain and customers in the demand chain is not enough. In today's business world, *coordination* is key. Business is working toward frictionless information flows, with information flowing to more places more easily.

Web-based technology affords the enterprise the ability to get more information to more places more easily. ERP technology affords an enterprise, its business partners in the supply chain, and its customers in the demand chain the ability to coordinate the information they have and to determine how they present it to others.

Processing logic is required in order to respond to information available across the Internet. For example, knowing the location and cost of raw materials is only the beginning of the manufacturing process. Raw material must be matched with manufacturing capacity and customer needs. As the value chain grows to involve more than a very few customers and manufacturers, raw-material algorithms must be applied to optimize the supply chain. The algorithms are available using ERP software, and Web-based technology supplies the information required to solve the equation. This is a perfect partnership.

Today's installed base of ERP is focused on integrating a business unit or integrating an enterprise. The integrated business unit focuses on providing customers with better products and services at lower cost. The integrated enterprise focuses on efficiency and flexibility across the organization and on speed of internal information flow. Tomorrow's ERP will be focused on integrating the extended, networked enterprise, which is beginning to emerge now, and which focuses on multienterprise supply-chain integration and growth.

E-NABLING TECHNOLOGY

Web-based technology is fundamentally cheap, easy to use, and easy to implement compared to previous generations of communication software. Its acceptance has been phenomenal because it is based on simple principles that provide a powerful basis for communication.

The Internet operates in much the same way as a language. The base components are sounds (through Internet protocol, or IP). When pronounced with care, sounds become distinct and recognizable as letters in an alphabet (HTML or XML). Letters can be combined into words (base data). Words become sentences (one-way electronic messages, like placing an order on a Web site). Sentences become dialogue when grammar is applied.

The best e-business is an electronic dialogue between two organizations, with little or no human involvement and effort. This dialogue is based on prearranged ways of working. Thus, the key to successful e-business is the ability to speak the same language and use the same grammar. Open standards provide the common language and grammar that make electronic dialogue possible.

OPEN STANDARDS

Whereas EDI technology is one-to-one, Web-based technology is many-to-many. Figure 2-8 illustrates the difference between these two concepts. Open standards provide hardware and software interoperability among many players. Open standards cost far less than proprietary EDI.

END-STAGE ARCHITECTURE

As companies adopt the open standards that subsume ERP into Web-based technologies, their systems architectures will change dramatically. Figure 2-9 depicts the end-stage system architecture for the

Figure 2-8   EDI and Open Standards

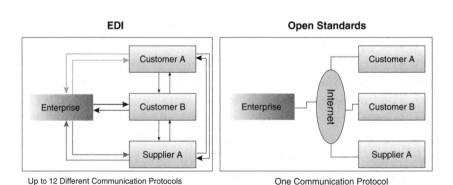

Figure 2-9   Twenty-First Century Systems Architecture

Customers   Suppliers

Trading Partners

twenty-first century company. At the center is the company's ERP system, which is its transaction-processing engine and generator of its internal data. This data, which is stored in a data warehouse, can be sliced and diced in any number of ways by the company's decision-support software, which may be part of the ERP package or may be provided by another vendor, and which the company uses to conduct business analysis.

With Web-based technology, the company can transfer information both to and from its customers, suppliers, and trading partners. In addition, Web-based technology allows the company to utilize Internet-based research sources to add richness and robustness to its business analysis. Decision-support technology assists managers at all levels of the organization to make coherent decisions by giving them a clear picture of relevant information from both inside and outside the company. In such a system, data from both internal and external sources can be consolidated and compared with a company's targets as part of the performance measurement system, in effect turning data into management information. As well as historical performance, a company needs to be able to consolidate forward-looking information, including budgets, rolling forecasts, and latest estimates.

To provide unbiased business intelligence and a sound basis for decision making, internal information must be viewed in context with information from external sources. With the Internet, accessing external information is no longer a problem. The challenge is to find the salient facts among the vast quantity of available data. Continuously changing, often unstructured, and typically qualitative rather than quantitative, external data is often difficult to filter and assimilate. In the past, without appropriate tools, many companies used external information in an informal, sporadic way. Today, the pace of business change makes a more systematic approach essential. And the Internet makes such an approach possible.

3

Web Economics: Valuing Your ERP and E-Business Investments

In the past, companies have made resource-allocation decisions based on the value of the money spent today compared to the potential money earned or saved in the future. But the truth about making these kinds of business projections is that it is much easier to calculate cost savings than revenue enhancements. This is because a company can exert much more control over its internal cost savings—either cost reduction or cost avoidance—than it can over how customers and potential customers will respond to the company's efforts to increase revenue.

Measurement of internal factors is appropriate for creating a business case for an effort that focuses on internal operations, such as an investment in an ERP system. However, because one goal of e-business is to connect with customers, it is necessary to find a new set of financial analytics in order to value and manage potential e-business initiatives. E-business has completely changed the basic nature of the interface between a company and its customers, and has changed the profit margins earned by companies throughout the entire value chain. The ubiquitous nature of information for customers has had a deflationary impact on prices.

Traditionally, there are three reasons a company can charge a premium price: new technology, lack of competition, or ignorance in the marketplace. E-business has done away with marketplace ignorance, reduced the barriers to entry for new competitors in many industries, and allowed companies to more effectively bundle information-rich services with products as a proxy for new products. All of this leads to an incredible possibility for new revenues. Yet, traditional financial analysis techniques fall short when it comes to valuing revenue-enhancing technology.

All companies need to make decisions about selecting and managing e-business initiatives based on a quantitative understanding of what delivers value to customers, business partners, and shareholders. They must answer three questions:

1. What is most important to our customers, business partners, and shareholders?
2. Which current or potential e-business initiatives have the greatest impact on customers, business partners, and shareholder value?
3. Are the current e-business initiatives meeting customer, business partner, and shareholder needs?

Customer-value drivers include superior product performance, reliability, service levels, competitive pricing, and the general ease of doing business with a particular product or service provider. The ability to deliver these value drivers consistently to business partners adds to brand value, which in turn results in trust and loyalty. Trust and loyalty add to the bottom line of every successful business in a way that is hard to measure and quantify.

What is the predictable, quantifiable result of an on-time delivery? What is the predictable, quantifiable impact on future business if the quoted price is wrong or if the delivery is late (or early)? E-business tools allow businesses to do a better, more consistent job on all of these value drivers. The difficulty is predicting and measuring their business benefit.

Traditional valuation approaches often result in an inefficient portfolio of e-business initiatives that do not take into account customer values or the value of options. These traditional valuation approaches, most notably payback period and discounted cash flow, are biased against customer-focused initiatives because of the level of uncertainty, and toward internal, cost-based initiatives.

Trying to use these static valuation tools on a dynamic, disruptive technology such as e-business too often creates a poor-performing portfolio of e-business initiatives and/or a mix of initiatives that is inconsistent with the enterprise's overall business strategy. The tendency is for businesses to take a short-term approach to e-business initiatives or projects because short-term outcomes are easier to predict and are considered to be safe bets in today's fast-changing environment.

The overemphasis on "low-hanging fruit" and the tendency to spread resources too thin creates a portfolio full of projects that do not deliver the maximum possible value to the enterprise. In order to properly value e-business initiatives, it is necessary to use a dynamic valuation tool such as real options valuation (ROV™), a proprietary PricewaterhouseCoopers tool that takes decision analysis and option pricing techniques developed by economists to the next level.

FIFTY YEARS OF VALUATION HISTORY

Sophisticated valuation analysis tools did not exist until the late 1940s. They were developed in response to businesses' need for a systematic and consistent way to compare different options in an increasingly complex environment.

The first and simplest tool provided a way to determine "payback period." Computing the payback period is straightforward. One simply determines how many months or years it will take for the profit (that is, decreased costs or increased revenue) generated by an investment to cover the initial cost of the investment. For example, if a company has an option to spend $1 million today, it might put in a new computer system or purchase manufacturing equipment to enhance a production line.

47

To support this decision, the payback period for each can be calculated. Investing in the computer system might provide $100,000 per year in cost savings, in which case the payback period would be 10 years. However, the equipment to enhance the production line might mean $200,000 per year in increased profit, in which case the payback period would be five years. Based simply on payback period, the production equipment looks like the better way to invest the capital. Payback period calculation was the key to capital investment decisions throughout the 1950s and 1960s.

Beginning in the 1970s, companies turned to the notion of discounted cash flow, which added to the payback period a cost of capital calculation and a calculation for the cumulative effects of inflation. In the high-inflation years of the 1970s, there was increased awareness of the fact that having $1 in hand today was better than having $1.05 a year from now. From this perspective, the financial decision is based on the future cash flows discounted back to the value in current dollars. This is called net present value (NPV), and performing this calculation is called doing a discounted cash flow (DCF) analysis.

Even if the company has cash to invest, in order to determine the payback period using DCF, it is necessary to determine how much the cost of borrowing the funds or raising the funds through equity would be. Typically, a company will use a discounted amount that is greater than its cost of borrowing or raising the funds—its cost of capital. In other words, the company will not use shareholder funds for internal investment unless that investment can generate a better rate of return than the company could get if it invested the funds on the open market. In static terms, it is not difficult to calculate how either inflation or cost of capital affects the payback period.

Another complicating factor in this calculation is the opportunity cost—the cost of the opportunities lost that would have accrued had the investment been spent in another way. Opportunity cost is very hard to calculate, however, and in a typical DCF calculation is often an ignored uncertainty.

Even in a seemingly simple cost-saving exercise, there is always some element of uncertainty, and DCF analyses are only as accurate as the estimation of future inflation and the cost of capital. A discount rate based on these is aggressive, and if an internal investment passes this so-called hurdle rate, then a manager can be reasonably certain that, based on performance, the investment will outperform both the stock market and inflation.

This margin seemed acceptable for a project in which the performance variables could be controlled, such as a computer system or production line installation, and when the time frame was short term and the investment results reasonably certain. But for decisions such as research and development (R&D) planning, or mergers and acquisitions, or new technology, DCF simply is not robust in its treatment of uncertainty.

Beginning in the 1980s, economists and business school corporate-finance faculty began looking at a series of techniques that might help better assess uncertainty and provide executives with a way to manage that uncertainty so that they might make bolder investment decisions. Two of these techniques—scenario simulations and decisions analysis—are used extensively by the U.S. Department of Defense. The third—option pricing—is an economic model designed to value the price of financial market options, based on an assessment of the probabilities of future uncertainties in stock price.

ROV™ consolidates this thinking into a new standard for evaluating, making, and managing strategic investment decisions. ROV™ makes sense when a large investment is being considered, when options can be created and exercised, when there is a lot of uncertainty about the future, and when there are complex and interrelated decisions with many alternatives. Companies need a rigorous tool to quantify the value of their e-business investments, given the magnitude of spending on e-business initiatives and the enormous options available to focus those efforts on customers or suppliers; on simply opening an e-commerce channel, integrating the value chain, or even trying to transform an industry through the use of e-business; and on developing potential new business models.

The growth in valuation techniques over the past 30 to 40 years can be seen as a change in approach to uncertainty. While

before 1970, uncertainty was ignored by simple payback calculations, today, when ROV™ is used, uncertainty is exploited. This
change is tracked in Figure 3-1.

TRADITIONAL VALUATION TECHNIQUES WORK
FOR ERP

Recently, an audience of about 125 chief financial officers of Global
1,000 companies were asked how many of those whose companies
had implemented an ERP solution had developed a true business
case for the investment. Only 35 percent had.

The ERP investment decision is based on answering four
questions:

1. Why do it?
2. How should it be done?
3. What are the costs?
4. What are the benefits?

Traditional valuation techniques are appropriate tools to answer these
questions because ERP is an investment in the internal operations of

Figure 3-1   Evolution of Valuation Techniques and Change in Attitude
                  toward Uncertainty

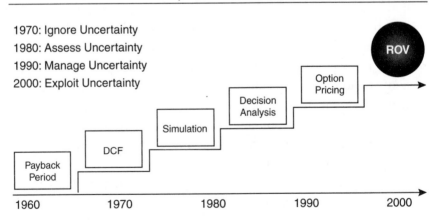

an organization, which should have a direct impact that either reduces cost or increases profitability.

Why Do It?

An ERP installation is a large investment of resources—financial resources for the cost of the software license and the outside assistance necessary to complete the implementation, as well as the company's own human resources.

Installing ERP also requires a lot of time—more than 12 months in most cases and up to 36 months or more in extremely large, complex companies that are simultaneously engaging in a high degree of process change. Multicountry implementations add to the burden. As Figure 3-2 illustrates, the complexity of an ERP implementation increases with the increase in the degree of process change. Figure 3-3 illustrates the timeline that should be considered for implementations with differing degrees of process change complexity. (There will always be exceptions to these timelines.)

Figure 3-2   Complexity Increases with Increased Process Change

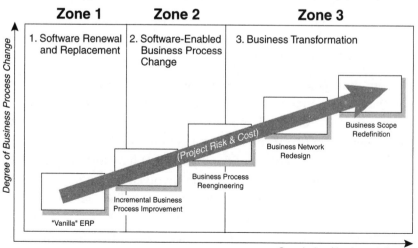

Figure 3-3   Approximate Time Frames for Process Change

Business Degree Process Change

	Zone 1 Low	Zone 2 Medium	Zone 3 High
High	12–18 months	18–36 months	24–48+ months
Medium	6–9 months	12–18 months	18–36 months
Low **(Vanilla ERP)**	3–6 months	6–9 months	12–18 months

Business Complexity (vertical axis label)

The only truly acceptable reason to engage in an ERP installation is as part of a corporate strategy, supported by a proper information technology strategy, and a business case that defines both quantifiable and nonquantifiable benefits.

How Should It Be Done?

This question gets at a number of issues. The first is one of degree. Will the implementation be integrated across the enterprise, across a single business unit or a few business units, or within a single function, either on an enterprise or business-unit basis?

Second is the question of deployment. Where and when will the system be deployed, and who will be involved in the deployments? Will an integrated enterprise installation be rolled out by business unit, by nation/region, or by process and function?

Third is the set of systems decisions. Which ERP system will be implemented? Does it make sense to implement more than one ERP package? Which business functions will be used from which package? How will the legacy systems be managed as the transition to ERP takes place? Will middleware be used? And so on. An overall systems architecture and plan is required to set the pace and vision for moving forward.

Fourth, and possibly most complex, are the organizational decisions. Overall, an enterprise must be realistic about determining whether it is ready for change. Or perhaps, more finitely, an enterprise must realistically assess how much change it can absorb over a given time period.

When implementing an ERP system across an enterprise or a significant component of an enterprise, many parts of the organization are affected. The way people work is changed, in many cases in a very fundamental way. The computer systems they use are different, and they require training; new code sets must be learned and the old ones forgotten. The flow of work is altered; new work pathways must be established and old ones blocked.

Most people in an enterprise view the changes created by implementing an ERP system as disruptive because of the difficulty of working in new ways. The problem individuals have in seeing or explaining why the benefits outweigh the difficulties is perhaps the most significant reason for the failure of some organizations to be fully successful with ERP implementation. Due to the integrated nature of ERPs, users must be educated about where they fit in the process flow.

What Are the Costs?

An ERP implementation involves two kinds of costs: quantifiable costs that lend themselves to a DCF analysis, and human-factor costs that are unquantifiable but very real. Quantifiable costs fall into five categories: hardware, software, training and change management, data conversions, and reengineering. As Figure 3-4 illustrates, the bulk of the costs involve human issues, process reengineering, and change management. When analyzing each of these costs, decision makers must assess which will be one-time costs and how long the duration of that time will be, and which costs will be ongoing.

Figure 3-4   Costs for ERP Implementation

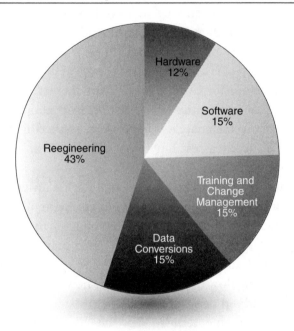

Source: AMR Research

Human-factor costs are hard to quantify, but they do have an economic impact. There are human-factor costs both to individuals and to the organization in general. Costs to individuals include career displacement for the duration of working on the project, project fatigue, and the decrease in a manager's capacity to manage. Because ERP implementation can take many years, an individual assigned to such a project will often not progress in his or her career within the company during this time. Additionally, such long time frames make it difficult for individuals to feel a sense of accomplishment, which can be demotivating (something we have come to know as *project fatigue*). Finally, the level of complexity and scope of such projects is often beyond the average manager's capacity to manage. What is the cost to the enterprise if, within the course of implementing an ERP system, a potential chief executive officer becomes burned out?

Other costs to the organization involve nonquantifiable costs to
the governance structure. An ERP installation affects both the power
structures within the organization and the company's usual decision-
making process. Access to information is often a key to control and
authority within an enterprise. Implementing an ERP system can
give far wider access to information. Recognizing this early on, managers and executives can begin a campaign to either control or termi-
nate the ERP implementation. The turmoil and time associated with
these types of activities cost the company, although how much is
hard to say.

What Are the Benefits?

Benefits of an ERP implementation also come in two varieties—
quantifiable and qualitative. Some of these are illustrated in Figure 3-
5. The quantifiable benefits are increased process efficiency; reduced
transaction costs due to the availability and accuracy of data and the
ability to turn that data into meaningful information; reduced information organization costs in hardware, software, and staff necessary

Figure 3-5   ERP Benefits

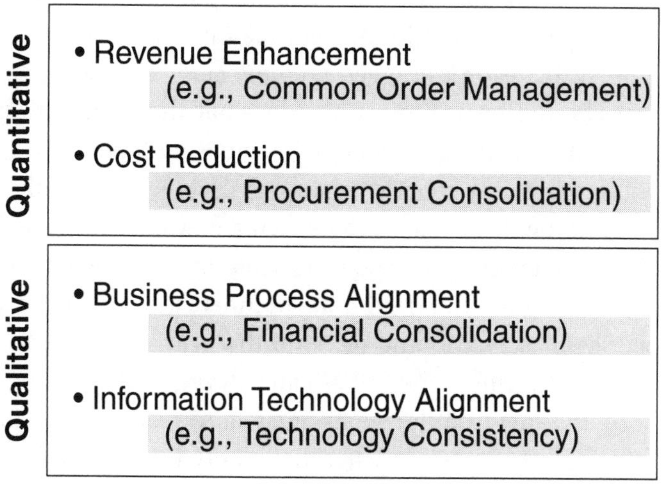

to maintain legacy systems; and reduced staff-training costs over time as people become more "change ready."

Qualitative benefits include a more flexible governance and organizational structure, and a work force ready to change and focus more on high–value-added tasks and to more easily capitalize on opportunities as they present themselves.

A NEW TECHNIQUE NECESSARY FOR E-BUSINESS

While traditional analytical techniques are appropriate to ERP, e-business requires an approach for balancing many projects against limited resources. ROV™ provides a way of quantifying the impact of the risks, uncertainties, and options associated with e-business initiatives and facilitates a more effective decision-making process.

ROV™ is both a strategic and financial analysis tool that is especially relevant to evaluating e-business opportunities because it values the uncertainties inherent in the e-business environment. DCF requires that the environment be certain and that the analyst be prescient in projecting future cash flows. ROV™ not only acknowledges that the future is uncertain, but it is based on a principle of future uncertainty.

An analogy with military strategy is useful. Traditional military strategy was once based on a static, one-battle approach (Figure 3-6). This approach assumed that there was a single possible way to fight the enemy in any given battle. But as we all know, once the first shot is fired, the battle becomes ragged and any static scenario falls apart. Almost always, the enemy does not do what the scenario planners thought it would do, and the strategy becomes useless.

Modern military scenario planning involves a set of options (Figure 3-7) and deploys resources in such a way that they are flexible and can be maneuvered to respond to what the enemy actually does once the battle begins. To be sure, the planners are still forced to pick one "most likely" scenario and develop the primary strategy around it. But properly executed, the forces can still respond.

Part of this new battle planning is a reconnaissance function (Figure 3-8), which scopes out what the enemy is doing and gives the

56

Figure 3-6   One-Battle Strategy

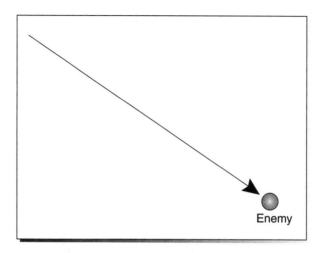

battle leaders the earliest possible warning about which scenarios to close down, helping to redeploy activity (i.e., resources) so that it remains flexible and can respond even more quickly to a narrowed group of available options.

Figure 3-7   Multiple Strategies: Pick One

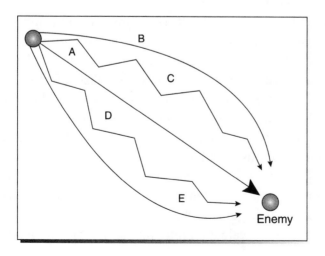

Figure 3-8   Multiple Strategies with Reconnaissance

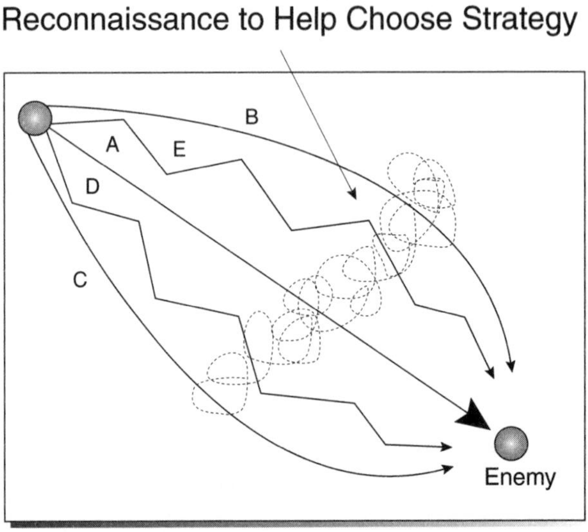

Reconnaissance to Help Choose Strategy

As with the old military strategy, most financial valuation methods consider only a single execution route to achieve value. DCF, for instance, does not incorporate uncertainty or management flexibility. However, conditions change over time, and management must learn and respond effectively.

ROV™ builds on DCF, decision analysis, and option pricing models to provide a more complete picture of the future. The primary tenet of ROV™ is that asset value is intimately linked to asset management. Figure 3-9 illustrates how, by utilizing ROV™, management can widen its horizon and analyze the many small risks encountered as it builds a portfolio of e-business initiatives. Each e-business project has the potential to go in many different directions at many different times over its duration.

ROV™ analysis helps explain a portion of the premium the financial markets place on companies that are heavily invested in e-business initiatives (Figure 3-10), explaining why pure dot.coms often command enormous valuation multiples and in fact often attain high

Figure 3-9   ROV™ Helps Management Widen Its Horizons

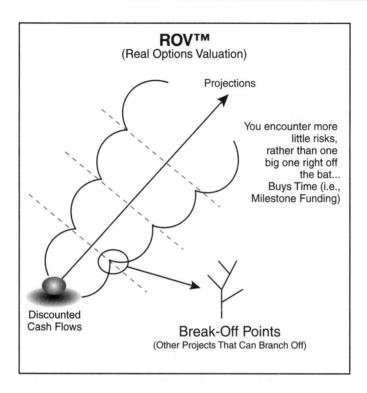

prices with no earnings history. For example, priceline.com is worth more than the largest U.S. airlines because it has moved beyond its original role as an on-line air ticket sales company to include hotel rooms, groceries, and more.

Analyzing how much of the market premium is due to the value of a dot.com company's business options and how much is due to pure market speculation is important in discussions of various relationships, from mergers and acquisitions and joint ventures to simple partnering in an extended enterprise. For example, for many months investors placed a huge premium on Amazon.com. One financial analyst said that for Amazon.com to command the valuation that it did based on the book business, the company would have to sell 90 percent of all books sold in the United States. The value, the analyst

Figure 3-10   Value of Options Helps Explain a Portion of Market Premium
for Companies Heavily Involved in E-Business

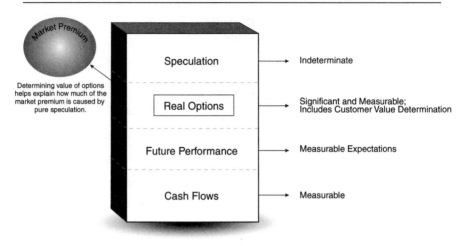

stated, was based on Amazon's options of being able to sell toys, compact discs, and so on, either alone or in partnership with bricks-and-mortar companies. That is exactly what Amazon.com began to do in 1999.

In addition, the following nonfinancial key performance indicators are critical in determining valuation:

o Ability to execute corporate strategy
o Credibility of management
o Quality of corporate strategy
o Ability to innovate
o Ability to attract and retain quality people.

However, at some point the market asks management to choose among available options and then to execute. While e-business allows a company to "buy time," leave many options open, and increase its options, at some point simply adding options is not enough. For example, Intel has investments in over 50 small, privately owned technology companies. Over time, it will probably divest 80 to 90 percent of those positions, either by selling out or through marketplace attrition. However, if five or ten of these investments pay off, the total investment will have been worth it because of the knowledge the company acquires about various technologies.

DOING THE ROV™ ANALYSIS

ROV™ involves five steps that enable management to capture the full impact of e-business initiatives on customer value and, ultimately, on shareholder value:

1. Assess
2. Frame
3. Analyze
4. Interpret
5. Implement.

Steps 2, 3, and 4 are key.

Framing

In this step, value measures and success criteria are laid out; risks, opportunities, and options are defined; and the key question of how value can be created is asked. We use a proprietary technique called Open Framing™, which creatively identifies the factors (uncertainties) that affect the future e-business environment, and the management alternatives (options) for anticipating and responding to them. One example might be anticipating the impact of mobile computing as an industry. In Norway, for instance, it is possible today to buy a soft drink from a vending machine using a cell phone to place and pay for the order. This is a boon to those who never carry change but always carry their phone.

The end result of open framing is a Dream Tree™ of the possible outcomes of e-business initiatives, including both the potential future decisions and the uncertainties (Figure 3-11). One important feature differentiates ROV™ from DCF. The more uncertain a project, the

Figure 3-11 Dream Tree

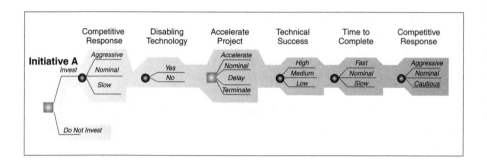

greater the value it may have, and unlike DCF, ROV™ can help calculate this potential value. With ROV™, an analyst can compute a
more refined set of discount rates than with DCF, and take into
account improvements in effectiveness as well as efficiency. To perform this calculation, the analyst plots a set of valuation maps that
measure the possible outcomes of many e-business initiatives against
a set of metrics (Figures 3-12, 3-13, 3-14, and 3-15).

Figure 3-12   E-Business Initiative NPV Range Based on Risks

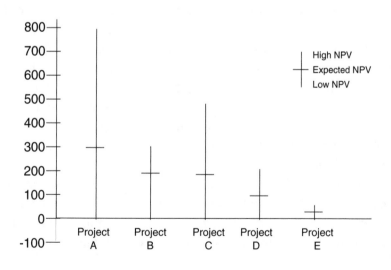

Figure 3-13   E-Business Initiative Success Factors for a Single Project

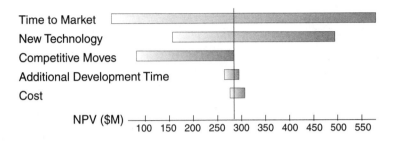

As Figure 3-16 illustrates, ROV™ is also a more robust portfolio analysis tool than DCF. With this methodology, an analyst can understand the cumulative value of the company's options in the context of the risk associated with each project.

Analyzing

Analyzing includes data gathering and modeling. The key question in this step is: What does the company need to know in order to create value?

Figure 3-14   E-Business Initiative Risk versus Reward for Each Project

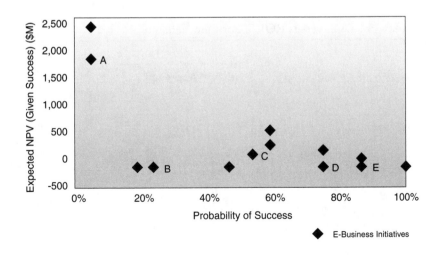

Figure 3-15   E-Business Initiative Portfolio Return and Risk by Year

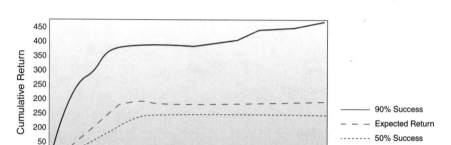

Analysts collect data and develop models to describe the evolution of uncertainties and decisions over time and to evaluate e-business initiatives from an investor perspective. In a process called market strategy advisory (MSA) analysis, they develop estimates of the customer value impact of e-business initiatives and translate them into revenue projections. MSA predicts future customer behavior and determines the impact on market share of a wide range of e-business initiatives. It adapts to the changing e-business environment and to changes in the competitive environment. In conjunction with

Figure 3-16   DCF versus ROV™ Portfolio Valuation

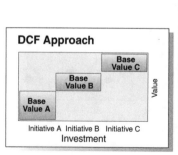

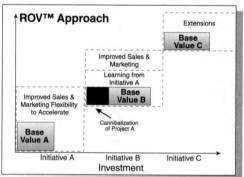

ROV™, MSA translates this learning into fact-based decision making. By focusing on fundamental customer needs, MSA is an ongoing tool that provides guidance for three to five years, even in dynamic, changing markets.

The MSA approach creates a "virtual customer panel" that models a customer's response to each e-business initiative and translates it into revenue projections. By using "what if" scenarios, a company's e-business offerings as well as prospective offerings of competitors, and primary research data on customer priorities, perceptions, and price sensitivities, analysts create a model of individual customer preferences and marketplace dynamics, which is then translated into market-share forecasts by product, customer segment, geography, and other variables.

Interpretation

With information created through the Open Framing™ and MSA analysis, a company can estimate the revenue impact of an e-business portfolio over time. From this, the company can select the dynamic management plan to achieve the highest return and predict resulting value.

Implementation

Implementation involves turning the various rank-ordered initiatives into real projects. To do this, one must have the end in mind. Often, e-business initiatives require a solid foundation. For example, establishing an e-commerce channel may be a first priority and necessary first step on the way to integrating the value chain.

MAKING THE RIGHT INVESTMENTS

Unless a company has a framework for deciding its investment priorities, it will have difficulty determining which options to pursue. A company must understand its mission and the key business imperatives necessary to achieve it. Applying financial analysis using tech-

Figure 3-17   Establishing Investment Priorities

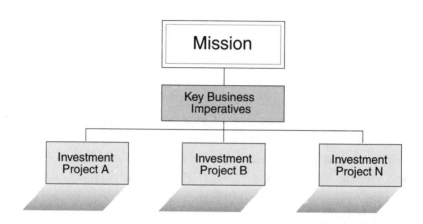

niques described in this chapter helps a company determine its priorities. This understanding guides how limited resources (for example, people and funding) are applied to the many potential investment projects available to a company. This cascading effect is illustrated in Figure 3-17.

For example, the key business imperative for a business-to-consumer company might be to build the brand. In this case, the emphasis would be placed on investments in projects that deal with the Web front end. Alternatively, a company with a business-to-business focus and a business imperative to deliver quality on time might make the bulk of its investments in integrating its materials requirement planning functionality with that of its business partners.

4

ERP/E-Business Matrix: Options and Scenarios

In Chapter 1, we briefly introduced the 5×5 ERP/e-business matrix (Figure 4-1). In this chapter, we will describe in more detail each of the five possible positions a company can inhabit along the ERP axis.

ERP SCENARIOS

The five possible ERP scenarios, or spaces, in which a company can operate are greenfield, nonintegrated systems, limited single-function ERP, integrated business unit ERP, or integrated enterprise ERP. In reality, a corporation may not map perfectly to any one of these spaces. The purpose of categorization is to create a framework within which to define both a company's current state and its desired state in order to formulate an ERP/e-business strategy.

Greenfield

A company with a greenfield ERP scenario is, by definition, a start-up company. No systems are in place, and the cultural impact of any decision to move to another ERP scenario is low. Once a company purchases its first computer and software package to help operate its business, it immediately moves to another ERP scenario. If that soft-

Figure 4-1   ERP/E-Business Matrix

	No E-Business Capabilities	Channel Enhancement	Value-Chain Integration	Industry Transformation	Convergence
Greenfield					
Nonintegrated Systems					
Limited/Single-Function ERP					
Integrated Business-Unit ERP					
Integrated Enterprise ERP					

ware package is not an ERP package, the company moves to the legacy systems scenario, albeit potentially as a "best-in-class" example. If that package is an ERP package, the company moves to one of the three possible ERP-based scenarios.

A start-up company today is well placed to jump immediately into e-business. Five key drivers move it in this direction:

1. In today's business environment, access to and speed of communication with the customer have taken positions of primacy. A company without an existing ERP or legacy system infrastructure has a tremendous opportunity to create a business based on speed and access to the customer.
2. The company must focus on the basic processes required to carry out its mission. Increasingly, these have to do with communication and information transfer. For a period of

time, e-business applications may have enough transaction-processing power to handle the workload. As the workload increases, some sort of ERP system will become necessary to handle day-to-day business transactions and to provide meaningful information based on those transactions.

3. Process or application outsourcing is an increasingly popular model that is making virtual companies possible. More options for purchasing ERP applications from a third-party application service provider (the ASP model) are appearing daily.

4. Early processes are often built to take advantage of the capability of the software purchased, rather than to solve actual problems. Once software is in place, human nature imposes a switching cost in the form of cultural adjustment and change management, no matter how flexible the work force. Furthermore, we now know that changing (or even upgrading) an ERP system can be a huge drain on both financial and human resources.

   E-business software can be relatively inexpensive when compared with ERP software, and the emerging dot.com work force is highly flexible, especially when it comes to utilizing new software. Start-up companies, therefore, have a clear advantage in flexibility over companies that have been around for a while. However, transitions are never frictionless. Even the cost of updating simple Web-based text is expensive.

5. E-business is essential to supply- and demand-chain management. This driver mitigates most of the culture change issues that do exist in a greenfield business.

It is possible, although unlikely, that a company operating in a greenfield ERP scenario will jump immediately to any one of the five positions along the e-business landscape—no e-business, creating an e-commerce channel, value-chain integration, industry transformation, or possibly even convergence. A company in the greenfield

ERP scenario is clearly in the best possible position to define an e-business–based business model. However, such a company cannot simply let the e-business world carry it along. If it is to reach its full potential, it needs to take five key steps:

1. Evaluate e-business alternatives. The choice of where in the e-business landscape the company wishes to be and when it wishes to be there may have an impact on whether it decides to go with an ERP or non-ERP transaction-processing system and, if it chooses an ERP system, which operating model it chooses.

2. Finalize an enterprise e-business strategy that supports the enterprise's overall business strategy.

3. Make an affirmative selection of an ERP- or non–ERP-based transaction-processing engine. An ERP engine can either be purchased, owned, and maintained by the company, or it can be one that runs on some sort of an outsourced model— either an ASP model or a company-owned and contractor-operated model.

4. Implement a unified ERP/e-business strategy. The focus should be on how benefits can be maximized.

5. Remember that e-business is not about technology; it is about strategic transformation. An e-business strategy must take into account how the company's internal systems will operate, as well as how it will interact with network partners up and down the supply and demand chains.

Nonintegrated Systems

A company operating in the nonintegrated (legacy) systems scenario is characterized by an environment that has a large number of nonintegrated information systems with many different hardware platforms and operating systems, numerous application programs, and competing computer languages. Some of these may be early packaged systems (late 1980s, early 1990s) that were installed in a nonintegrated fashion, as well as systems that were, in the past, considered best in class, or custom-designed systems.

Many of these information systems are unique to a particular corporate function. For instance, a separate system runs accounts payable (AP); another runs accounts receivable (AR); and a third runs human resource (HR) information. Still others run manufacturing. This state of affairs reinforces functional silos within the company and breeds significant cultural issues. Interfaces are required to bridge data-access limitations and to allow the various systems to "talk" to one another. Typically, an enterprise exchanges data between systems with batch interfaces that keep the system synchronized on a daily, weekly, or monthly basis. Data warehousing is required to bring the data from different systems together in a consolidated view that provides meaningful information and allows management to make decisions that steer the enterprise in the right direction.

Such an environment has enormous ongoing maintenance costs for both interfaces and integration solutions, and might be characterized as "worst in class." For a company operating in such an environment, there are four key drivers and areas of focus:

1. *Maintaining all of these legacy systems.* Knowledge of how these systems operate internally is often lost as personnel move on and documentation is not updated. System maintenance becomes increasingly complex as new changes are applied on top of earlier changes, and technical support of these systems can become impossible as tools to support them become outdated and unsupported.

2. *The high redundant costs of such an environment, in terms of both systems and staff.* Compilers, operating systems, and even the physical machines themselves must be kept operational long after they would normally have been decommissioned, in order to ensure that these systems continue to operate.

3. *Inter-entity issues.* These affect business units or even cross-functional organizations. Many of these show up in financial reporting, including inventory, pricing, and eliminations.

Simply put, keeping these systems in balance creates a lot of manual work.

4. *The difficulty of creating consistent and meaningful reports in such an environment.* Because the job of getting consistent data across these systems becomes increasingly difficult with time, management reports become skewed, with mismatched data that, in the worst cases, can lead to the wrong business decisions.

For such a company, e-business might be viewed as a panacea— a way to fix the system without having to actually fix its pieces. Such a company might hope to link whatever transaction processing power exists in various e-business front ends in an effort to camouflage the disparate systems that exist internally. A tempting road to e-business for such a company is to hide behind Web-based customer front ends in an attempt to cover up infrastructure deficiencies. This may, in fact, increase back-office exposure and cost.

Linking various front ends to different ERP and legacy systems has a high cost, does not assist with back-office integration, and may actually limit the company's ability to rid itself of legacy systems. Organizational costs increase, and freezing legacy systems in place may make it impossible for the company to move into the industry transformation or convergence snapshot of the e-business panorama.

Such a company is in danger of having customers "two-click" them out of existence. The first click is to the company's Web site. When the customer cannot get the benefits promised by the Web site because of poorly integrated back-office systems, the next click will be to a competitor.

For example, if a company's e-business strategy is to develop new sales channels through Web-based technology, the back-office systems will be stressed to provide real-time/accurate data regarding product availability. Customer expectations will be set regarding delivery and quality of products. If back-office systems provide inaccurate data about availability or cannot reserve product to a specific sales order, the potential to disappoint customers is enormous!

A company with multiple legacy systems may not be able to migrate further than the e-commerce channel without stepping back and putting resources into an ERP solution. For this company, the action items are:

○ Finalize an ERP, enterprise, and legacy decommissioning strategy. Determine whether a final ERP solution will be integration at the business-unit level or at the enterprise level.

○ Determine an e-business strategy, including where in the e-business panorama the company would like to play, and develop a resource allocation plan to coalesce ERP and e-business efforts.

○ Select an ERP technology. Determine whether initial e-business efforts will be undertaken prior to, in conjunction with, or after the work on ERP. Because the ERP system is larger, more costly, and less flexible than e-business front ends, the Web-based technology should be aligned with the ERP technology, rather than the other way around. Business strategy should ultimately drive the use of Web-based technology.

Some companies in the legacy environment may determine that the best way to get into e-business is to strip down their product line and refocus, such as the Swedish company Ericsson did in the mid-1990s, moving from being a large, diversified manufacturer to a maker of mobile telephony equipment. Others may decide to carve out a separate business unit for e-business in order to create a new business model from a greenfield position. General Motors did this in creating its Saturn division.

ERP Integration Depends on Corporate Organizational Model

A company's place in the ERP/e-business matrix is determined by whether it operates as an overall enterprise (centralized) or autonomous business units (decentralized, or holding-company model). Generally, an overall enterprise organization has an integrated value chain across business units (that is, each unit consumes products made by the other units in the enterprise, and end products are offered to the customer). Separate ERP systems add to the complexity of such an environment, especially in the areas of intercompany activities of the integrated demand/supply chain. This organization will have great difficulty with ERP if it tries to act as a holding company and in fact is not. For example, a pharmaceutical company may have three factories. At one, it manufactures compounds from raw materials. At a second, it makes tablets and capsules from the compounds and bottles them. At the third factory, it conducts packaging and shipping.

A holding company is made up of business units that are, in effect, independent businesses that are operated independently of each other (with no integrated products). These business units may effectively use separate ERP solutions, with the enterprise ERP solution at the business-unit level. An enterprise solution for this type of organization may not be required in order to achieve benefits of both ERP and e-business, especially if their customers are different.

Limited/Single-Function ERP

In this scenario, a company's ERP systems are installed to operate in a single functional area across a business unit, such as finance or sales and distribution, or across the enterprise. Such an ERP implementation may have multiple ERP systems from multiple vendors across the company. Human resources, procurement, finance, sales, and distribution are examples of functions. In effect, this is similar to a legacy system environment, except that in the corporate functions in which ERP systems have been installed, these systems are a generation or more newer than many of the legacy systems we have been discussing. Also, ERP, even by function, eliminates the custom systems and many of the interfaces written to bridge custom and legacy systems.

However, access is limited to functional areas, and interfaces and data warehousing are still necessary to bridge data access limitations and to integrate either ERP or earlier legacy systems. Single-function ERP does nothing to eliminate the inter-entity issues of inventory, pricing, and eliminations, or financial or management reporting issues. There are still redundancy costs for both systems and staff.

In the ERP-by-function scenario, company organization is not terribly important because the lack of integration between ERP modules negates benefits achievable from an integrated ERP, regardless of whether the organization is centralized or decentralized. As with the legacy system environment, companies in the ERP-by-function scenario may view e-business as a panacea. A company in the ERP-by-function scenario, with e-business front-end systems in place, is like a swan gliding across a lake. The customer sees it gracefully gliding by. But underneath the surface, the company, like the swan, is paddling fast. It has to in order to move information among disparate ERP systems.

As with the company in the legacy system scenario, a company that utilizes ERP by function uses the front end to the customer in an attempt to hide back-office deficiencies, although these deficiencies are not as severe as those of companies with non-ERP legacy systems. The same front end is used to communicate with multiple ERP and legacy systems. Organizational costs are still high, and there is still a limited ability to eliminate legacy systems. Companies with an ERP system for manufacturing may get to the value-chain integration snapshot of the e-business scenario. But if manufacturing is still in the legacy system environment, a company in the ERP-by-function scenario is probably stuck in an e-commerce channel because it will be difficult to integrate its legacy systems with its business partners' systems.

Like legacy system companies, ERP-by-function companies must decide how to allocate resources between ERP and e-business. They must finalize both their ERP and enterprise strategies based on whether they will operate as independent business units or as business units integrated into enterprises.

Finally, they must allow their choice of ERP systems to drive their choice of Web-based technology. Because the company has clearly spent resources implementing one or more ERP systems in various functions, questions of cost and desire come into play.

The tendency of many, both at the operational level and the executive level, will be to ask two questions that reflect their skepticism: If past ERP expenditures have not solved the problem, can incurring more costs to upgrade or reimplement ERP solve them? And if ERP did not work, why not try e-business? The wrong answers to these questions can ultimately result in customer dissatisfaction and limit future possibilities. What has changed are the dynamics of a new business model, and technology must adapt to enable that change.

Integrated Business-Unit ERP

In this scenario, end-to-end processes are integrated within individual business units. Minor legacy system issues within a business unit may exist along with issues of inter-business-unit legacy systems and integration. Even with integrated ERP at the business-unit level, inter-entity issues such as inventory, pricing, and eliminations; inter-business-unit supply- and demand-chain issues; and redundant costs in terms of systems and staff may still persist. With ERP by business unit, the company can begin thinking of the issues it will encounter in inter-business-unit value chains and extended enterprises.

Companies in this environment will still need to deal with e-business and cross-business-unit legacy system issues. These will mostly revolve around the "one face to the customer" question: Will Web-based front ends work together or individually? For example, if the enterprise with an integrated supply chain has not had the rigor to implement an integrated ERP solution, the company will most likely have approached e-business in a fragmented way, with multiple e-business solutions on the horizon. The internal stress caused by lack of concurrence on common processes that the company faced when implementing an ERP will still exist when it approaches e-business, but this stress will be more visible to the customer.

This company can use consistent front-end technology to hide the reality of multiple business units from the customer (for example, a Web solution that, through catalogs or interfaces, effectively hides the nonintegrated solution from the customer). Having multiple ERPs by business unit will mean additional organizational costs, making the total greater than those in an enterprise-wide ERP system. However, industry transformation and convergence are possible in this ERP scenario, especially where one business unit is transforming an industry or its niche in an industry.

A company operating in this environment finds it easy to work in the e-commerce channel, and individual business units would be able to integrate value chains to form an extended enterprise. Such a company would have as its major action step confirming its enterprise strategy, whether it wanted to stay decentralized or move to the enterprise ERP scenario.

If the enterprise chooses to stay decentralized, individual business units can develop their own e-business strategies, but to get the most gain from e-business, the company should seek to make uniform the design of the Web pages customers see, in order to provide one face to the customer, and to simplify development and support. After determining the proper e-business solutions, each business unit could implement its back-office connections on its own timetable.

If the company chooses to pursue an enterprise ERP outlook, it needs to develop an enterprise strategy, select an ERP solution (possibly choosing as a model the business unit that has done the most with its ERP solution), refine e-business alternatives (again looking to the business unit that has pursued e-business the farthest), and finally implement both the ERP and e-business strategies.

Integrated Enterprise ERP

Any integrated enterprise ERP solution must be well run. If the ERP solution is not well run, it is more costly to maintain and upgrade than legacy systems because of the direct impact of changes in an integrated system. A well-run integrated enterprise ERP environment involves end-to-end processes throughout the company, global process owners, common data elements across business units, and standardized ERP application software, with a single set of applications applied across the enterprise.

Access to data and information across the enterprise is efficient and timely, and only minor legacy system issues exist, if any at all. In such an environment, transaction costs are low, and all of the company's resources can be put into e-business solutions that utilize the enterprise-wide ERP. Within such an environment, the company can be truly customer focused, because it does not have to spend resources either hiding back-office problems from the customer or trying to improve back-office operations to meet customer expectations. Costs can continue to be lowered.

Continuous improvement in the internal value chain can be extended to provide continuous improvement across the supply and demand chains. Partnerships and consortiums may be optimized into extended enterprises. Such a company can make optimum decisions about establishing shared service operations, and possibly even selling its shared services as an outsourcer of such activities to others. It can also become the hub of such services to the members of the extraprise and move toward a virtual production environment.

A company with a fully integrated ERP across its enterprise can look to its current ERP vendor to provide front-end technology, use the third-party front-end technology that best integrates with its ERP technology, or acquire the best-in-breed front-end technology and then make it work with its ERP technology. Such a company has the ability to play in any of the e-business snapshots. It has the ability to become the lead participant in an extended enterprise and to manage a group that will go to market as a value network. This company's action items include finalizing its enterprise strategy, evaluating its e-business alternatives, and implementing the most appropriate e-business alternatives.

Of course, a company whose ERP solution is not "well run" must focus its resources on optimizing the use of its ERP application suite. As with other ERP scenarios, a poorly run enterprise integrated ERP system can easily result in customer dissatisfaction due to insufficient or inaccurate information.

SHARED SERVICE CENTER CONSIDERATIONS

In a shared service center, a company consolidates all of the activities from a general category such as payroll, accounts payable, or customer service from multiple offices of a single business unit, or from multiple business units in an enterprise, into a stand-alone operating unit. Although shared services may sound like centralization, it is actually a boon to decentralization.

Shared service centers carry out support-process activities. By removing the need to manage these support processes, business-unit executives have more time and resources with which to manage their core business processes, the ones that assist in carrying out the business unit's mission and strategy. Eventually, the shared services can be outsourced if further cost-saving can be achieved.

Having an ERP system in place enhances a company's ability to carry out shared services. Web-based technology can also be utilized to make existing shared service centers more effective and as another incentive for creating shared service centers where they do not already exist.

TIME AND COST

The ERP scenario a company is playing in, as well as how well the ERP solution is operating, determines to a great degree the time it will take to implement an e-business strategy and the cost of that implementation (Figure 4-2). The more fragmented the environment, the more costly it is to implement e-business solutions. (The exception to this is the empty greenfield environment.)

If the process and integration issues were not effectively addressed in the ERP implementation, they will need to be addressed at this time. Ignoring ERP and attempting to address only the integration deficiencies in an e-business solution will most likely only add to the company's overall ongoing costs. The company should assess correcting the end-to-end processes within an ERP solution and align the e-business strategy around the corrected processes. Companies that will achieve the greatest benefits from

Figure 4-2   Time and Cost to Implement E-Business Solutions Starting
from Different ERP Scenarios

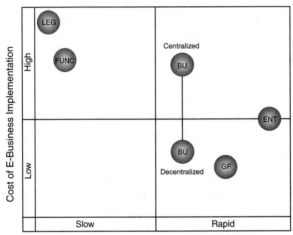

e-business will be those that have a foundation in ERP solutions that enhance the company's ability to process the e-business transactions efficiently, with minimal intervention. These companies must have an ERP system integrated at least by business unit, if not across the enterprise.

Without this integration between the Web and the company's ERP solution, the cost of doing business will be compounded by ongoing maintenance and upgrade costs to keep the environment functioning. It is never too late to balance the use of ERP with emerging e-business opportunities in order to achieve and support the extended enterprise across the Internet.

5

Behind the Web: Supply-Chain Management

Discussions about e-business often focus on the Internet-based link to the customer. However, a company's bottom line is far more dependent on what is behind the Web page than on what is on the Web page. Many companies are missing out on significant cost savings and revenue opportunities by focusing only on the customer-facing applications of e-business rather than the improvements that an integrated electronic supply chain can bring to day-to-day enterprise-wide operations. The current fervor of customer-focused solutions is driven by fear of losing market share. The back-end integration of customer applications, so critical to the overall success of the application, is too often overlooked.

A company's value chain sits behind its Web page. The value chain encompasses an array of business processes that create value by delivering goods and services to customers. Regardless of whether a company produces and delivers a physical product or a service, it has a value chain.

Broadly, a company's value chain consists of product planning, procurement, manufacturing, order fulfillment, and service and support (Figure 5-1). A vertically integrated company extends its control of the value chain as far back as possible, quite literally to "own" the

Figure 5-1   Simple Value Chain

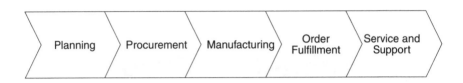

raw materials that are used in its products. For example, some large oil companies control the product from well head to pump handle. In other cases, companies may choose to focus on a core competency or set of competencies and let others manage and run various parts of the industry value chain.

Reasons for choosing one business approach over another vary from industry to industry, company to company, and each company's particular strategy. What is common to all industries is the power of Web-based technologies to significantly change the status quo by providing a mechanism that further integrates the value chain. A highly integrated value chain creates greater value for the end customer by delivering products and services more efficiently and effectively. Within the industry value chain, the group of companies that carry out each step in creating and delivering product is called the supply chain.

E-SUPPLY CHAIN

Electronic supply-chain management (e-SCM) is the collaborative use of technology to enhance business-to-business processes and improve speed, agility, real-time control, and customer satisfaction. Not about technology change alone, e-SCM is about cultural change and changes in management policies, performance metrics, business processes, and organizational structures across the supply chain.

The success of an e-supply chain depends on two major factors. First, all companies in the supply chain must view partner collaboration as a strategic asset and a "must do" in terms of operational priorities. It is this tight integration and trust among trading partners that generates speed, agility, and reduced costs. Second, information visibility across the supply chain can become a substitute for inventory; therefore, information must be managed as inventory is managed today—with strict policies, discipline, and daily monitoring. Speed, cost, quality, and customer service are the metrics by which supply chains are measured. Consequently, companies must clearly define their value in the supply chain and their attractiveness as business partners.

Integrating the supply chain more tightly, both within a company and across an extended enterprise made up of suppliers, trading partners, logistics providers, and the distribution channel, is the vision implied in the second snapshot of the e-business panorama, value-chain integration. Figure 5-2 illustrates the flow of information to and from customers and suppliers, with the enterprise as the hub.

Figure 5-2   Enterprise Process Flow

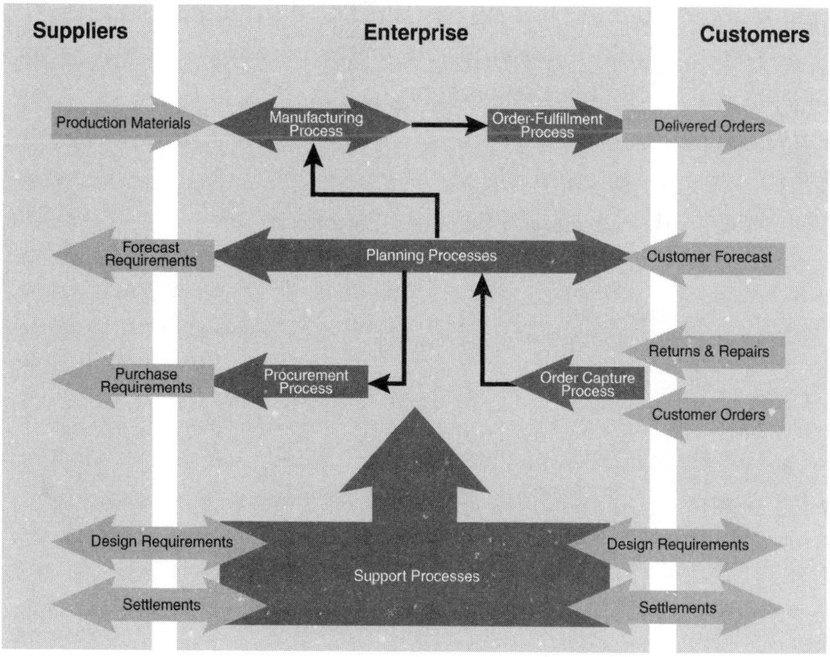

Over time, extended enterprises will supplant individual companies as the entities that compete against one another. Extended enterprises with the shortest time to market, the most agility, the highest degree of synchronization, and the lowest cost will dominate markets because customers will naturally select them. These trends, however, do not negate the power of product differentiation or diversification. Figure 5-3 illustrates how third-party business partners feed into the simple value chain to form an extended enterprise.

At the core of value-chain integration is visibility, access, and timeliness. Essentially, value-chain integration allows real-time synchronization of supply and demand. The enabler to support an organization in its efforts to become part of an extended enterprise, e-SCM requires companies to develop collaborative business systems and processes that can span across multiple enterprise boundaries.

According to Forrester Research, value-chain integration is where most companies are pursuing performance improvement opportunities today. Forrester estimates that by 2001, over 70 percent of companies will be sharing demand, inventory, and order-status information with their trading partners and distribution channels.

Figure 5-4 illustrates all of the pieces necessary to create a successful value-chain integration effort.

Figure 5-3   Value Chain with Extended Enterprise

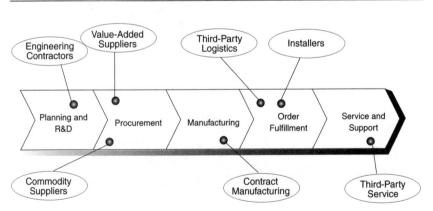

Figure 5-4   Components of Value-Chain Integration

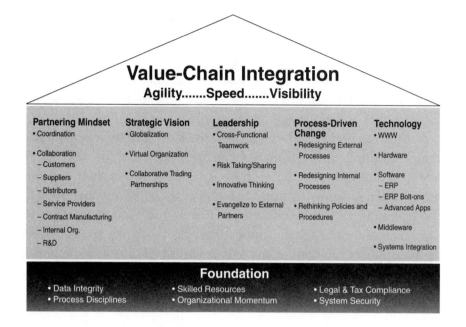

SIX COMPONENTS OF THE E-SUPPLY CHAIN

The e-supply chain consists of six components:

1. Supply-chain replenishment
2. E-procurement
3. Collaborative planning
4. Collaborative product development
5. E-logistics
6. Supply webs.

Supply-Chain Replenishment

Supply-chain replenishment encompasses the integrated production and distribution processes that utilize real-time demand and strategic partner alignment to improve customer responsiveness. Supply-chain replenishment is a natural extension of Web-enabled customer orders.

Companies can use this information to reduce inventories, eliminate stocking points and distribution steps, and increase the velocity of replenishment by synchronizing supply and demand information across the extended enterprise. Real-time supply and demand information facilitates make-to-order and assemble-to-order manufacturing strategies across the extended enterprise.

Much as on-line orders eliminate intermediary steps in the traditional ordering process, manufacturing policy can be altered by adopting assemble-to-order or make-to-order strategies. In the assemble-to-order situation, strategic inventory can be placed just prior to the operation to which the order is directly routed upon receipt. In the make-to-order scenario, manufacturing processes are tightened up so suppliers can react to the live order in real time and the physical process can begin.

E-Procurement

E-procurement is the use of Web-based technology to support the key procurement processes, including requisitioning, sourcing, contracting, ordering, and payment. E-procurement supports the purchase of both direct and indirect materials and employs several Web-based functions such as on-line catalogs, contracts, purchase orders, and shipping notices.

On-line catalogs can be used to eliminate redesign of components in product development. Visibility of available parts and their attributes enable quick decision making. On-line purchase orders expedite the agreement, while advanced-shipping notifications and acknowledgments streamline delivery. Benefits include reduced processing costs, purchase price leverage, contract compliance, and improved delivery and quality.

Collaborative Planning

Collaborative planning requires buyers and sellers to develop a single shared forecast of demand and a plan of supply to support this demand, and to update it regularly, based on information shared over the Internet. Collaborative planning is a business-to-business (B2B) workflow across multiple enterprises over the Internet, with data exchanged among them dynamically.

Key component, manufacturing, and distribution partners all have real-time access to point-of-sale or order information. Partners create initial forecasts and provide changes as necessary, share forecasts so all parties work to a schedule aligned to a common view, and have access to order and forecast performance that is globally visible through electronic links. Schedule, order, or product changes trigger immediate adjustments to all parties' schedules.

Collaborative planning is designed to synchronize production plans and product flows, optimize resource utilization over an expanded capacity base, increase customer responsiveness, and reduce inventories.

Collaborative Product Development

Collaborative product development involves the use of product-design and product-development techniques across multiple companies, using e-business to improve product launch success and reduce time to market. Product-development costs can be reduced by tightly integrating and streamlining communication channels and design standards.

Once a product has been identified and defined, Web-based search engines can be used to identify existing technologies that fill a need. During development, engineering and design drawings can be shared over a secure network among the contract house, testing facility, marketing firm, and downstream manufacturing and service companies.

Other techniques include sharing specifications, test results, and design changes, and using on-line prototyping to obtain customer feedback.

E-Logistics

E-logistics is the use of Web-based technologies to support the warehouse and transportation-management processes. E-logistics enables distribution to couple routing optimization with inventory tracking and tracing information. Internet-based freight auctions allow spot buying of trucking capacity. Third-party logistics providers offer virtual logistics services by integrating and optimizing distribution resources.

Supply Webs

At some time in the near future, supply webs will emerge as alternative configurations to the traditional supply chains. Information, transactions, products, and funds will all flow to and from multiple nodes on a supply web to satisfy customer demand. Supply webs will form as trade exchanges or portals appear to serve industry sectors by integrating the supply-chain systems of various buyers and sellers, creating virtual trading communities.

These are already emerging in various forms. For example, i2 is teaming with various partners to promote the TradeMatrix product; large oil companies are selling via on-line energy marketplaces; and the Big Three automakers expect to do hundreds of billions of dollars of business with their suppliers in a new on-line exchange due to operate by 2001.

THREE PHASES OF SUPPLY-CHAIN INTEGRATION

Forrester defines three stages of supply-chain integration: integration, extension, and exploitation.

In the integration stage, companies create an integrated view of their own supply chain by linking disparate ERP and legacy systems into one comprehensive data set. In turn, this data set feeds advanced planning systems that enable a company to respond rapidly to changes in either supply or demand.

In the extension stage, companies use Internet technology to begin working together in bidirectional, real-time data sharing arrangements with suppliers, trading partners, and logistics providers. For companies to take full advantage of the opportunities provided by Internet technology, they will need to implement process, organizational, and cultural changes. For some companies, these changes can be dramatic.

In the exploitation stage, companies utilize their relationships to become more agile. Developing technology standards reduce both information-sharing costs and the costs of switching partners. This, in turn, pushes apart many long-standing relationships and forces suppliers to compete continually on price and service.

Through all of these stages, trading partners who have invested in ERP are particularly well suited to leverage e-business investments to achieve true value-chain integration. Cutting-edge companies are in the extension phase and will, by 2002, be in the exploitation phase. If a company is not at least in the integration phase by 2001, it will probably be on its way to extinction.

ADVANCED PLANNING AND SCHEDULING

Advanced planning and scheduling (APS) system functionality ranges from strategic (network optimization) and tactical (supply planning) to operational (line scheduling). Most APS systems use mathematical algorithms (such as linear programming) to identify optimal solutions to complex planning problems that are bound by such constraints as materials, labor, or capacity resources.

APS systems are particularly well suited to solving the challenges associated with supply-chain management for three reasons:

1. They focus on critical constraints such as machine capacity.
2. They provide modeling to run different scenarios and "what-if" analyses.
3. They highlight exceptions and recommend a course of action.

APS applications are decision-support systems designed to develop an optimization plan for a production line, plant, or overall supply chain. They receive and process data from other databases and transaction-based applications such as ERP systems.

Why Are APS Systems Needed?

The combination of globalization, shorter product life cycles, and greater product variation makes it more important than ever that companies maximize the effectiveness of their supply chains. While ERP systems have within them the ability to integrate the information flows within supply-chain activities, ERP planning logic is based on the logic of manufacturing resource planning (MRP II). APS software provides a better way of managing supply-chain activity information flows.

Supply-chain planning software is about 30 years old. Materials requirement planning (MRP) software, introduced in the early 1970s, was the first planning software. Companies quickly realized that MRP calculations were based on a set of faulty assumptions: that all customers, products, and materials are equally important; that lead times are fixed; that all resources are infinite; and that all elements of the supply chain will deliver the required quantity on the required date. Simply put, MRP did not deal with the reality of the production environment.

Another large flaw with MRP calculations is that they are conducted as a batch process, typically taking hours to run. MRP calculations had to be run on nights and weekends, making it difficult for managers to implement necessary changes during normal working hours.

MRP II, which came on the scene in the mid-1980s, added some functionality, improving inventory control and high-level capacity planning. Although there was some real-time feedback for managers, most MRP II calculations still took hours to complete. Many companies developed their own one-off planning software solutions, but these were often as cumbersome and ineffective as MRP and MRP II. Many corporate planners find ERP to be "more of the same, only faster."

Companies as varied as Ford in motor vehicles, Black & Decker in hand tools, Coca-Cola in beverages, and Frito-Lay in snack foods have used APS tools to transform their supply-chain management. These tools are provided by specialty software companies like

Manugistics, i2, Chesapeake, and Red Pepper (purchased in 1999 by PeopleSoft).

Companies using APS software have reduced inventory between 20 and 70 percent, lowered cost by up to 12 percent, and trimmed capital by up to 15 percent. More important, however, they have increased sales due to better customer service by between 2 and 15 percent; improved production throughput by 2 to 6 percent; and increased customer response, at lower total cost.

But quantifiable results of APS software offer only one advantage. APS is also a key enabler of process and behavioral change. With APS, the production organization can move from being functionally based to being process driven. Unplanned emergency orders can be handled more effectively. Planners leverage knowledge better and make better decisions. And the production organization can adapt quickly and effectively to changing customer requirements.

While many companies have reaped some or most of these benefits, others have failed to do so. Both supply-chain optimization and the APS systems to achieve it are in their infancy. Many companies do not need APS technology to plan production, and many companies cannot yet afford the technology. As these systems become more robust and less expensive, they will more firmly take their place in the information systems portfolios of more and more companies.

What Does APS Provide?

While the purpose of APS systems is similar to that of any other planning software—to deliver 100 percent service to customers while minimizing costs to the company—they distinguish themselves from ERP planning software in that they allow managers to manipulate the supply chain in real time. The software provides value in three main areas:

1. Constraint-based planning
2. Real-time processing
3. Integration.

While MRP and its successors deal with multiple constraints simply by providing a planner with exception reports, APS software weighs all of the constraints, including materials, labor, machines, warehousing, and logistics, and suggests optimal planning scenarios to balance those constraints in order to provide the highest level of customer service at the lowest cost to the company.

Unlike fast MRP, which sought to marry the latest processing technology to conventional MRP logic, APS utilizes such techniques as linear programming to enable "real-time" calculations to assist decision making. And while MRP-based planning tools consider one aspect of the supply chain at a time, APS systems are modular in nature and can be constructed to provide a truly integrated solution to the problems of supply-chain management. The various modules can be installed individually or in any combination that provides advantage to the company. Many companies find they can install two to four modules that are particularly important in their industry and be well on their way to achieving lasting results.

ERP and APS

Now that companies' information technology organizations are finished with their Year 2000 (Y2K) and European monetary union work, optimizing the supply chain will become the next area to explore to gain competitive advantage. The ERP companies know this, and they know that to date the APS providers have far better solutions than theirs. Some will form alliances with APS software providers, such as the alliance between Oracle and Manugistics. Others, like PeopleSoft, will purchase APS providers and integrate the APS software into their portfolio of ERP modules.

ERP AND E-BUSINESS "SUPERCHARGE" EACH OTHER

When ERP and e-business are properly implemented, each one supercharges the other. E-business is the best vehicle to share business information with trading partners, which in turn creates major business-to-business synergies. The types of information shared among companies include demand forecasts, inventory status, order status, capacity availability, new-product information, product change information, design data, drawings and specifications, and financial information. The accuracy, consistency, and timeliness of this type of data directly determine the success of the processes the data support. A well-implemented ERP system is the best way to create and capture this type of data. Good data are the foundation of the e-business world, and ERP systems provide good data.

The current focus on e-business results from business's instinct for intimate customer relationships. It is also driven by an untapped capability to develop and deliver products and services fast; extend geographic reach; increase process efficiency and effectiveness; redefine products, services, and brands; and leverage information by providing more flexible infrastructures and business models.

However, companies that try to integrate within an extended value chain before implementing their own ERP systems will find the benefits of value-chain integration to be elusive. Without ERP, e-business may do nothing more than create both upstream and downstream problems at Internet speed. These problems result from lack of reliable, accurate, and timely information that trading partners require, as well as from the inability to make intelligent decisions and take effective action on the newly available information coming into the company from suppliers and customers.

The company that has the strongest internal ERP systems may become the de facto network master of the extended enterprise to which it belongs. In the same way that companies in the past sent out people from their own factories to assist suppliers with total quality management or just-in-time manufacturing techniques, the network master may send out specialists to assist suppliers with their ERP so that the systems can work more closely and more fully utilize e-business. Companies that have solved data integrity and integration issues through their use of proprietary, electronic data interchange (EDI) technology may, in fact, be able to more quickly become a Web-based extended enterprise. Sorting out problems related to data integrity and to the process of exchanging data is more difficult than installing Web-based technology.

ERP AND VALUE-CHAIN INTEGRATION EQUAL LARGE-SCALE E-BUSINESS

A well-running ERP system makes value-chain integration that much more powerful. Several cases that illustrate this relationship involve successful early adopter companies such as IBM, Compaq, Adaptec, Dell, Thomson Consumer Electronics, Intel, and Cisco in high technology; the major U.S. automotive companies; Bank of America and Charles Schwab in financial services; and Amazon.com, Travelocity.com, and priceline.com in the retail industry.

Once a company's Web page is established, product and service information is available, and secure e-commerce transactions are in use, then the next step could be to integrate this information with suppliers. A place to start in integrating the value chain is to develop Web-based collaborative planning and forecasting capabilities with customers to enable future demand to be shared, and then to extend this collaboration to suppliers so that the extended end-to-end supply chain can be synchronized daily as demand and supply information changes.

Businesses will increasingly persuade their trading partners to connect to the extended enterprise. Big companies will pressure trading partners and suppliers and freeze out those who do not e-trade. When companies trade this way, they collaborate more closely in terms of supply-chain planning. They share data about their planned needs to allow their suppliers the opportunity to work with them more closely to meet customer demand.

A number of new business models are beginning to appear and will become stronger over the next few years. These include:

○ *Infomediaries,* which consolidate buyers and sellers in fragmented markets. Travelocity.com is an example in the travel world, providing airport, hotel, and rental car information to buyers on-line, and representing a host of different sellers.

- *Aggregators,* which pull together fragmented markets for buyers. Ariba is such a company. Ariba works in the e-procurement world, aggregating the products of dozens of nonproduction supply companies and produces e-catalogs customized to the buying company. Individuals within the buying company can buy only from those companies whose products are in the intranet-based catalog. Orders are consolidated at the buying company and sent to Ariba via the Internet; Ariba forwards orders to individual companies and disaggregates the payment from the buying company to all of the selling companies.
- *Auctioneers,* which provide reliable channels for sellers. Auctioneers are very popular in business-to-consumer (B2C) e-business, eBay being the most well known. In the B2B world, they provide a way for companies to sell excess product and, in the future, may be an important way for companies to buy commodities. CheMatch and ChemConnect are providing this service to the chemicals industry. The Oracle B2B exchange service is well positioned for this role.
- *Exchangers,* which match bid and ask prices as a neutral third party on a stock exchange model.

Over time, B2B infomediaries will increasingly be able to transform industries. Power will shift to buyers as product and price information becomes more available and widely used. As more companies enter networks, the cost of changing suppliers will be reduced. Transaction costs and cycle times will also become compressed. Speed, range, accessibility, and low cost of information will create opportunities for more competition.

Although ERP vendors missed the first round of e-business, they will be major players in the second round. ERP vendors are beginning to market Web-enabled buy and sell applications as part of their suites. They will also make their current suite of applications more compatible to third-party front ends. This will help create a clear path for companies with ERP already installed. They will share a common information system with their customers. ERP will be extended into the systems of customers and suppliers using Web technology to create an extended and integrated value chain.

As dot.com companies grow larger, the most successful will be those with ERP backbones and systems discipline. Industry transformation will occur when large numbers of companies are extended into the e-business network. Highly successful companies will have reengineered their business processes during their ERP implementations to be more customer-centric.

Companies that are focused today on effectively running their businesses based on accurate, timely, and consistent data provided by well-implemented ERP systems are well positioned to be leaders in tomorrow's economy.

6

Customer Relationship Management

Companies are increasingly waking up to the fact that they can create wealth (new value) by working creatively with business partners in the distribution chain and with consumers to reduce costs and cycle times of products, and to provide better order-tracking information to customers. Customer delight is the key to enhancing revenue. Research has shown that only delighted customers are truly loyal. Delighted customers keep coming back. Providing a relationship that is merely satisfying, as opposed to delightful, leaves a company vulnerable to losing customers to a competitor with whom the customer finds it easier to do business.

Using information technology (IT), nimble companies can strengthen customer relationships by integrating sales, product configuration, planning, and design processes with customers through existing and new channels. Typically, a company has a set of preferred customers, but welcomes orders from any qualified buyer. Since the industrial revolution, companies have viewed orders as nothing more than demand for their product or service. As the source of revenue, customers are treated with respect, in hopes of getting repeat business.

Since the mid-1990s, customer information systems have empowered companies to capture data about customers in hopes of identifying unique buying attributes or trends. However, not until the application of the Web were businesses operating in a mass-production world able to truly personalize relationships with customers. The ability to build strong relationships with customers is causing renewed efforts among businesses to achieve lifetime value from current customers and to put strategic plans in place to go after lifetime value for new customers in new markets. In the world of e-business, companies can replicate the personal customer relationship that existed prior to mass markets by using knowledge of the customer to personalize customer service while continuing to sell standard products.

Customer relationship management (CRM) helps companies achieve this objective. The CRM application enhances the company's "front office," focusing on sales, marketing, and customer service. However, in order to be truly successful, CRM must be seen as a combination of people, processes, and systems, rather than as a narrowly defined IT application. CRM is one piece of the new wave of ERP that focuses on outward-facing processes, tying them together with the inside-the-enterprise transaction-processing engine of the original ERP systems.

WHY IS CUSTOMER RELATIONSHIP MANAGEMENT ON THE AGENDA NOW?

Identifying the importance of customers in the value chain is nothing new, nor is sales-force automation, or general database marketing. What is new is the technology available today. Technology today permits a far greater degree of sophistication in how sales and marketing interact with customers. In the past, marketing people have not generally been IT literate and, consequently, have not led the changes in their organization's IT infrastructure.

Now, however, with ERP systems in place in many organizations, the backbone exists on which to build CRM systems. Where ERP itself, with its focus on transaction processing, may have failed to deliver the anticipated benefits, CRM systems can provide tangible and measurable returns, centered on customers—sources of value creation.

Technology now exists that enables companies to conduct one-to-one marketing. These tools, frequently available off the shelf, are both powerful and inexpensive. They have transformed the selling and marketing landscape. Unlike some traditional forms of advertising, which are undirected and unspecified, CRM systems enable companies to communicate with customers on a personal level.

A company performing CRM provides a single corporate face to the customer, wherever the customer may encounter the company: through different business units, regional offices, or operational organizations within the company. Customers expect integrated, seamless, multichannel customer service that is transparent, whether the service is being provided by the company or by a third-party service provider.

The "new marketing" hinges on four key technologies: technology-enabled selling, call centers, e-business, and data warehousing/mining. In many instances, these technologies are combined to provide a seamless customer-service experience. Recognizing these emerging products, ERP vendors are now investing a great deal of money to catch up. But from the marketing world's perspective, they have a long way to go. As a result, in many areas, companies are using best-of-breed packages with bolt-on interfaces to their existing ERP systems. (Currently, a debate is taking place about whether best of breed or integration is best.) CRM packages are available that bundle many existing sales and marketing functions—such as sales-force automation, call-center systems, and data mining—with a robust technical architecture, resulting in integrated CRM with wide functionality.

TECHNOLOGY-ENABLED SELLING

Technology-enabled selling (TES) goes beyond the blind application of raw technology and deals with understanding the ways technology benefits the bottom line. The changing face of sales is speeding the drive for TES. In consumer markets, customers already expect a range of channels that offer consistent service. In the business-to-business (B2B) world, the new focus on relationships and the rise of the consultant-salesperson have increased complexity and diversity.

Managerial concerns around TES include determining just how TES will improve sales, how it can be implemented successfully, and how the company can overcome sales-force resistance. Often, the sales team does not see the opportunities for increasing sales, forcing the company to focus on cost and administrative savings.

Implementing TES is not just a matter of technology; rather, it requires creating new processes—supported by technology—that integrate customer information and transaction data, and that are informed by the company's strategy for improving revenues. Implemented properly, TES drives a broad range of benefits that reduce payback periods to, in some cases, less than 18 months, especially when the factors that increase revenue are taken into consideration. In addition to actual revenue increases, some "soft" improvements can occur. These include a clearer and more consistent marketing message, improved customization of marketing information, better cross-fertilization of market intelligence, and enhanced coordination across account teams.

Sales teams are better able to negotiate because of improved product and customer knowledge. Customer responsiveness improves, as sales teams find it easy to raise issues and help the company increase service, thereby building customer loyalty.

From a technical perspective, TES differs from other systems in many ways. A high level of integration is required with legacy systems because many companies choose to let the main transactional solution dictate the TES solution. Because TES often operates over disparate hardware systems, integration and interfaces are necessary to manage data consistency. Telecommunication links also need to be as high quality as possible.

TES has three sets of component building blocks. The first is a foundation of customer information located in company databases and manipulated either by legacy or ERP systems. The second is an infrastructure of systems that allow the company to communicate and transact business with customers; these employ telephones, faxes, personal computers, and other devices. The third is a set of advanced applications that are often specific to industries or sectors.

CALL CENTERS

Call centers are rapidly emerging as a means to provide service to customers, business partners, or employees. Increasingly, they are the main point of contact for customers. Call centers perform the following five functions:

1. Resolve issues or refer problems to the next level of service provider
2. Provide more information about products and services
3. Make recommendations to customers about the product or service that best suits the customer's needs
4. Take calls and monitor progress on customer requests and problems
5. Generate reports for root-cause analysis.

The best call centers link voice, video, and data into a comprehensive system to provide cutting-edge "customer care." A call center system and process must be constructed with the customer in mind.

Examples of successful call centers abound. Dell Computer does over $1 billion of sales through its Web site and through a call center located in Bracknell in southwest England, near Heathrow Airport. Polaroid runs a successful call center in Glasgow, Scotland, for after-sales service. Customers across Europe call a local or national toll-free telephone number. The computer software at the call center identifies the country the call is coming from and automatically routes the call to a customer service representative who speaks that country's language.

Call centers often have a three-tiered environment:

1. Technological screening
2. Service representative
3. Specialist or case manager.

This environment drives speed and consistency, facilitates self-service, optimizes resource utilization, and provides the necessary level of expertise when it is needed.

At all levels, call centers must have certain *information attributes,* including accuracy, confidentiality, accessibility, and reliability. At the first tier, they must have *technological attributes,* including intelligence, efficiency, controllability, and a human interface. At the second and third tiers, they must have *personal attributes,* including helpfulness, knowledge, responsibility, and comprehensiveness.

The quality of a customer's contact with a call center goes levels beyond e-mail or Web forms. Web-based customer service technology now includes Internet telephony and alternatives such as interactive text chats and callback requests.

E-NABLED CALL CENTERS

Today, most customers must talk to an account representative or navigate a seemingly endless spiral of voice recognition systems to get product or service information or order status. In the e-nabled company, customer-centric information systems are engineered around customer information touch points.

Web-based CRM is still in its infancy. While current systems provide capability for one-to-one marketing and rudimentary streamed video and sound, they are still mostly focused on push marketing with transaction processing.

Tomorrow's B2B customer experience will be far more exciting, providing more personalized value-added information than the customer would normally think to ask for, and supplying links to other related sites that complement the customer's interest and buying experience.

INTERNET PROTOCOL TELEPHONY

Frequently integrated into a preexisting call center, Internet protocol (IP) telephony in Internet call centers allows customers to speak directly with call center agents while using the browser to access the company's Web site. IP telephony can be used in call centers when, for example, a user is on a corporate Web site and requests technical support. The user clicks on a call button displayed on the Web page. The call button is a hypertext link that activates the IP telephony software, which then connects the user with a call center agent. If the customer enters his or her customer identification number, the call center agent can access the customer's history—the products the customer is using and the problems the customer has encountered previously. This access also enables the agent to sell upgrades or new products, based on the customer's purchasing history, and is enabled by computer-telephone integration (CTI) technology, which is available as a feature of high-end CRM software from such providers as eFusion, Ericcson, and Sitebridge.

As an alternative to IP telephony, a customer with two telephone lines can supply the second phone number to a merchant. While online, the customer can submit a request for support and expect a call on the second line. Callbacks are also used in situations in which the customer is protected by a firewall that does not permit IP telephony.

FIELD SERVICE

E-business customer service also enhances field service, which is the part of customer service in which qualified representatives of a company are sent to the customer's site to resolve problems. A call center can forward an unresolvable problem to an internal or external field service organization. E-nabled field service helps sales representatives by providing them with up-to-date customer and product information (including design documents and repair manuals) via the Internet. Field service representatives can check on outstanding customer queries, view their active service calls, and even update the status of accounts while traveling.

Cisco Systems has saved millions on Web-initiated customer service requests, and customer service productivity has increased dramatically. Sun Microsystems, a global provider of workstations, has created SunSolve, a service that allows customers to download product documentation and communicate with other users. A database is also provided to answer product questions. Using this and other e-customer services, Sun saves millions annually in software mailing costs and telephone support. Harley-Davidson does not expect consumers to buy motorcycles over the Internet. But the company does expect dealers to take advantage of the technology. Like many companies, Harley-Davidson is using e-business to enhance its existing dealer channel and help dealers provide better customer service, rather than trying to cut dealers out of the equation.

DATA WAREHOUSING AND DATA MINING

As the volume of data held by companies has grown, the focus of database management technology has shifted from data input to information output. A data warehouse consists of a highly cataloged and structured organization of company data in a knowledge repository in order to ensure that users, especially managers, have access to the right information at the right time.

The agent of transformation is a company's ability to leverage information, as opposed to traditional agents of change, like enhanced ability to manipulate physical product in a production cycle. The data warehouse is the enabler of change and, in the hands of a savvy company, can be the transforming element in an industry.

A data warehouse is the repository for a company's critical marketing and customer service decision data. In this respect, data warehousing represents a logical extension of decision support system models that preceded it. The data warehouse is a special-purpose database of preprocessed (indexed, partitioned, or preaggregated) operational data extracts from a company's databases, which are usually many and varied. By organizing data from various databases effectively, the data warehouse provides an orderly, accessible repository of known facts and related data that are used as the bases of inference and knowledge discovery.

Data warehouse systems enable end users to "mine" the historical data to identify trends and opportunities. A data warehouse offers easier and more timely access to key information by making the fullest use of the data resources available within and outside the company. Data warehouse systems allow a company to leverage the power of existing internal corporate data to improve customer marketing, to streamline business operations, and to better understand and forecast their financial position. The value of data warehousing lies in its ability to help users make more informed and faster decisions, without a great deal of effort in identifying the available data.

7

ERP/E-Business Impact on Shared Services

Before the Internet, the business case for shared service centers (SSCs) focused on cost savings through efficiency—reducing the costs and effort necessary to support many portions within the enterprise by consolidating activities that all parts of the business have to conduct, such as financial transaction processing, procurement, data center operation, desktop computer maintenance, or human resources benefits transactions. Web technology, however, reorients the business proposition for SSCs in three ways:

1. It shifts the focus from mere efficiency to increased effectiveness. Internet- and intranet-based communication technology extends the range of services the SSC can provide. For instance, a greater range of financial reporting, more human resource services, and more current information can all be provided via the Internet and company intranets.
2. Web technology may change the nature of the SSC itself. There may very well be no "C" in SSC—it will be virtual, a tightly integrated network of support that does not physically reside in a single location.
3. The SSC may become a separate business that provides services to outside businesses. It could become a strategic tool

107

offered selectively to preferred business partners, or simply a profit-making extension of the enterprise. It could also possibly be used to attract and retain business partners within an extended enterprise.

CONSOLIDATE, COMPACT, AND DISMISS

ERP and e-business utilized together enhance the utility and broaden the scope of SSCs. At a recent conference for SSC leaders, the vision for SSCs in an e-nabled world was explored. The key question asked was: Will e-business expand or eliminate shared service centers?

The group concluded that both will happen over a period of time. The technology inherent in e-business eliminates many activities that formerly were consolidated into SSCs. But for every set of activities that can be eliminated, another set is waiting to be brought in. Shared services collects and consolidates activities that are not strategic to a business, activities that no person really wants to do; then it compacts those activities, streamlining them for efficiency; and finally, using Web-based technology, those activities are automated and eliminated.

E-procurement offers a good example. E-procurement technology such as that offered by Ariba or Commerce One allows a company to make available to every employee on the company intranet a catalog of all the nonproduction (maintenance, repair, and operations [MRO]) goods that can be purchased, such as office supplies and equipment. Employees order their own goods; the system collects those orders and sends those that need approval to the proper individual, and then forwards the consolidated orders to the proper vendors for fulfillment.

Before e-procurement technology, MRO procurement—one of the noncore processes that was often consolidated in an SSC—was a paper transaction process with heavy human input. Today, technology has automated 90 to 95 percent of this process. Approvals alone require human intervention.

The automation of MRO procurement and elimination of that process from the SSC could justify closing down the SSC or bringing into it other complex processes and activities that require large amounts of human interaction. It should be seen as an opportunity to expand the scope of activities that fall within a shared service environment (Figure 7-1).

Clients at a recent conference conducted an analysis of what a company should do if it had not yet created an SSC: Should it do so before or after instituting an e-procurement effort? Should it simply utilize automation tools on decentralized processes and not have them pass through an SSC at all? The consensus was that e-procurement should be implemented first, and the activities that still exist in the e-procurement world (for example, approvals) should be consolidated.

In all of our discussions about shared service operations, we have made the argument that the goal of shared service management should be either to work itself out of a job over time (by streamlining processes to the point where they are so easily managed that they can be handed off to a provider of outsourced services in a simple relationship) or to create an operation that is so skillful the operation itself becomes a provider of outsourced services. The move to e-business does not change our mind; if anything, it reinforces our ideas about shared service management.

Figure 7-1   Scope of Shared Servive Centers Expands with E-Business

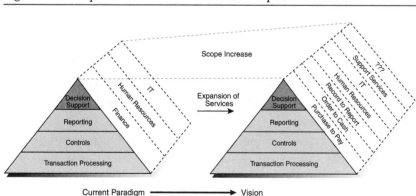

NATURE OF SHARED SERVICE CENTERS

Corporate support services are tactical. They are necessary and help support corporate strategy. Consolidating these nonstrategic processes and activities into a common organization under its own management frees managers within individual business units to manage and enhance their core competencies and strategic business processes, leading to enhanced customer value for the business unit's product or service and, ultimately, increased shareholder value.

SSCs are a way to offload support processes from all of the company's business units. Transaction-oriented support processes, such as those found in finance and accounting or human resources, are prime targets for this kind of consolidation. While the implementation of an SSC must be tailored to each company and its organizational structure, a common definition of shared services is possible. According to our definition, the shared services concept is:

> The concentration of company resources performing like activities, typically spread across the organization, in order to service multiple internal partners at lower cost and with higher service levels, with the common goal of delighting external customers and enhancing corporate value.

Sharing services does not imply centralization, nor does it imply a "corporate" mentality, in which services are located at corporate headquarters and in which the business unit takes what it can get and lives with it. In a shared services environment, service providers can be centrally located in centers of excellence or physically embedded into each business unit. In whatever form, however, SSC personnel report to the shared service organization's management. Finally, a shared services environment fosters joint accountability for cost and quality, through service-level agreements (SLAs), which stipulate price and performance.

Shared services can be implemented in a business unit or an enterprise (depending on the company's organizational structure) and operated in a single country, regionally, or even globally, depending on the complexity of the process and the company. For instance, British Airways has consolidated all of its customer service activities into three global customer service call centers—in Asia, Europe, and the United States. While no single call center runs 24 hours per day, one center is running at all times, providing customers with 24 × 7 customer service. With Internet capabilities, SSCs can now run on this voice center model as well, and companies are considering 24 × 7 global finance and other SSCs.

To Insource or Outsource

Any discussion of creating a shared service operation includes the following question: Why not outsource the consolidated activities and save the costs associated with running the operation? In fact, many companies decide to outsource these activities. Shared services and outsourced activities are flip sides of the same coin. Whether to outsource or "insource" into a shared service operation is the final question to ask after all of the data has been collected and analyzed.

The three key considerations for deciding whether to outsource or insource are:

1. What is the strategic relevance of the activities?
2. What is the current service level of these activities within the company as they are provided today?
3. What will the future required service levels of these activities be?

Each of these questions can be analyzed as a 2 × 2 matrix: relevance versus capabilities; cost effectiveness versus service levels; and required improvement over time versus required new products or services (Figure 7-2).

Let us take relevance versus capabilities as an example. If in-house capabilities are low, the presumption is to outsource rather than insource, regardless of the degree to which the company's oper-

Figure 7-2 Deciding Whether to Outsource

1. What is the strategic relevance and impact of the service?
   - Operational dependence on existing capability
   - Importance of sustained, innovative capability development

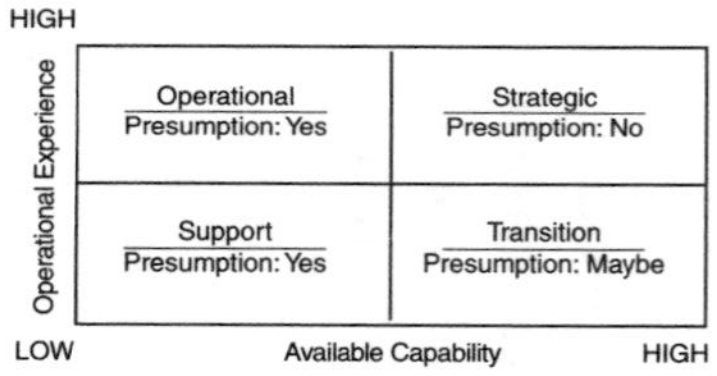

	Available Capability	
Operational Experience (HIGH)	Operational — Presumption: Yes	Strategic — Presumption: No
(LOW)	Support — Presumption: Yes	Transition — Presumption: Maybe
	LOW	HIGH

2. What is the current performance of this service?
   - Cost effectiveness
   - Service level

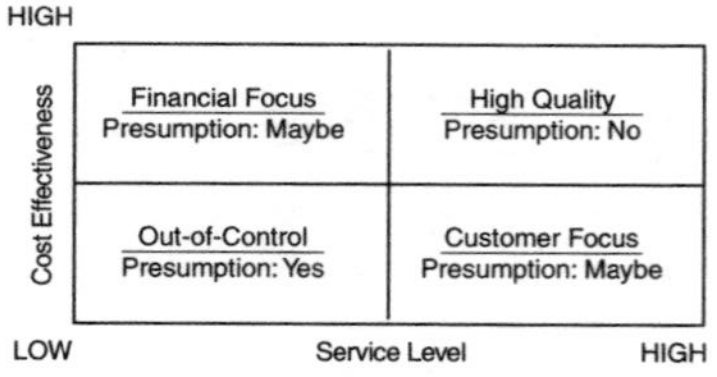

	Service Level	
Cost Effectiveness (HIGH)	Financial Focus — Presumption: Maybe	High Quality — Presumption: No
(LOW)	Out-of-Control — Presumption: Yes	Customer Focus — Presumption: Maybe
	LOW	HIGH

3. What will the future requirements of this service be?
   - Required improvement
   - Required new services, products, technologies

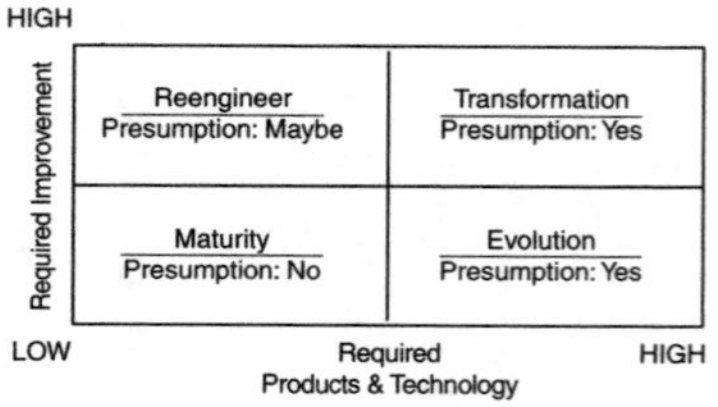

	Required Products & Technology	
Required Improvement (HIGH)	Reengineer — Presumption: Maybe	Transformation — Presumption: Yes
(LOW)	Maturity — Presumption: No	Evolution — Presumption: Yes
	LOW	HIGH

ations are dependent on the activity. If in-house capabilities are high, and there is a high degree of strategic relevance, the activities should never be outsourced. If capabilities are high and strategic relevance is low, a judgment call is required that hinges on whether the capabilities can be used in some other way to add more value.

Another key reason to insource rather than outsource is to maintain flexibility. This will be increasingly important, as transaction processing becomes Internet enabled.

ERP IS IMPORTANT FOR SHARED SERVICE CENTERS

ERP software allows companies to operate highly effective SSCs. In fact, a number of companies, including Bristol-Myers Squibb, Microsoft, Chevron, and Hewlett-Packard, combined successful implementation of ERP software with the creation of SSCs. With ERP software, a transaction need be entered only once. The software then records the transaction on all of the appropriate modules in the suite, resulting in a comprehensive, integrated support system, based on timely and accurate information. ERP systems deliver the information necessary for SSCs to operate. Without the internal flow of information, SSCs would not be able to support a business, especially a global one, within acceptable time and quality parameters.

A host of other technological tools can be used to enhance the ERP system and its ability to enable the shared service operation. These include imaging technology, automatic faxing, automated messaging, workflow management, and Internet requisitioning.

Workflow management is a way to group tasks into packets and send those packets to individuals who work on them. Automated messaging has a number of applications, among them internal auditing of quality. The system can be set to send messages to supervisors, managers, or inspectors when product is outside present tolerances or is "irregular." Imaging technology can be used to "see" documents without shipping them, satisfying both company needs and country regulations that documents not leave the country.

Such a system permits the handling of massive amounts of transactional information rapidly and with minimal human interference. Building such a process to take advantage of the latest technology not only leads to major cost savings, but creates an easier transaction for the end user.

ALTERNATIVE SHARED SERVICE CENTER SCENARIOS

Non–e-nabled SSCs are regional consolidations of back-office activities (Figure 7-3). E-business opens the door to three potential alternatives to these basic scenarios:

1. Integrated front and back office
2. Separated front and back office
3. Virtual SSC.

Integrated Front and Back Office

The model illustrated in Figure 7-4 indicates a number of front- and back-office processes consolidated in a series of regional SSCs or a

Figure 7-3   Regional Back Office

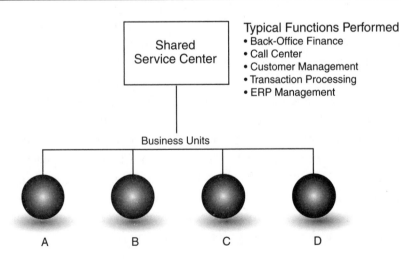

114

Figure 7-4   Integrated Front and Back Office

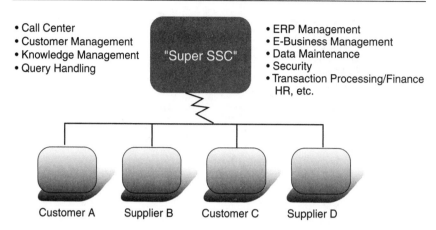

global "super SSC." These processes include front-office customer relationship management or "customer care" activities (call centers for inquiries, ordering, help, and service), the front-office "employee care" elements of human resources, the back-office activities involved in systems management, data maintenance, finance, and human resources management.

Separated Front and Back Office

In this model (Figure 7-5), front-office activities are maintained in a live mode, while the back-office activities are automated and maintained in a 24×7 lights-out mode. Both front- and back-office operations can be regional or global.

Global availability can also be maintained with regional operations, in a "follow-the-sun" mode. This is the case with American Airlines, which has customer-service centers in Asia, Europe, and the United States. While no center is active for more than 12 hours per day, customers have 24×7 access. A late-night telephone call from New York may be handled by the Asian center, or an early-morning call may be handled by the European center.

Figure 7-5   Separated Front and Back Office

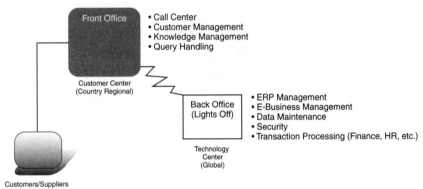

Virtual Shared Service Center

In this model (Figure 7-6), Web technology is used to create a virtual front office and a parallel virtual back office. Virtual SSCs will utilize application rental, telecommuting by staff, automated language routing to fluent help personnel, and a host of other technologies.

In reality, one "virtual" model will not dominate SSCs. Instead, hybrids will emerge, designed according to the process characteristics and the scale of the organization, in terms of both the shared service organization and the corporation. Differences in models will exist, depending on whether the services provided are transactional in nature or more decision support oriented.

Examples of different transaction models include:

- ○ A common model implemented on a regional basis, such as a European SSC, where processes are standardized but where there is still a level of real-time dialogue between the SSC and its partners.
- ○ A common model implemented globally, such as one global SSC, where processes are standardized, but real-time dialogue between the SSC and its partners does not occur. This is

Figure 7-6   Virtual Shared Service Center

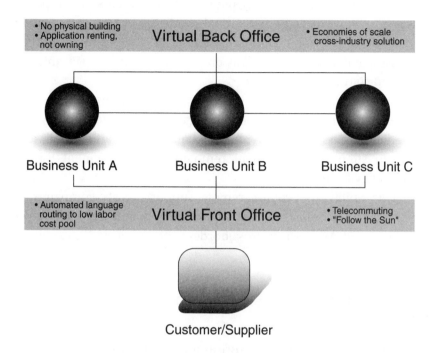

Customer/Supplier

applicable where one language is standard throughout the industry—such as in the airline or financial services industries in which English is the global language—or where software can handle the language issues.

○ A common model implemented on a devolved basis, such as staff operating from home or small units. This model is likely to be totally automated by such tools as workflow management. Time-and-attendance and performance indicators will also be managed electronically. This model is highly specific to each company.

Factors influencing the preferred solution will include the internal scale achievable, the potential to combine with other organizations, a decision to outsource or to become a provider of outsourced services, and the availability of language software to assist the process and the level of query handling required in the process. A company's ability to evolve directly to a virtual model or to take intermediate steps will depend on the consistency of the existing culture, processes, and systems, as well as on pressure from new entrants that can jump-start to a new model.

In general, decision support can go virtual more quickly than transactional processes. Intranet and data warehouse technology give immediate access to data. With videoconferencing and e-mail, analysts can support management remotely and supplement this by travel to key locations.

This ability to provide remote support assists companies in meeting the personnel retention challenge, which is especially acute in Europe and Asia, where cross-border mobility of staff is expensive and difficult.

EXTENDED ENTERPRISE SHARED SERVICE CENTERS

The creation of extended enterprises adds a new wrinkle to the idea of making an internal SSC "good enough to sell." A number of companies that have opted for internal SSCs over outsourcing now have best-in-class capabilities. These companies could use their SSCs to compete on the open market as third-party outsourcers for other companies. But many have decided not to turn their SSCs into stand-alone profit centers.

In the world of extended enterprises, such an internal capability can benefit business partners by allowing them to outsource a particular set of business process activities to one partner's SSC or by carving out the shared service organization as a stand-alone process outsourcer with an integrated set of clients—the extended enterprise members.

8

Triple Play: Technology, Processes, and People

Moving to an e-business environment involves a major organizational change. For many large, global companies, becoming an e-business is the fourth or fifth major organizational change they have undergone since the early 1980s. Many companies have gone through one or more rounds of business process reengineering (BPR); installation and major upgrades of an ERP system; upgrading legacy systems to be Y2K compliant; creating shared service centers; implementing just-in-time (JIT) manufacturing; automating the sales force; contract manufacturing; and the major challenges related to the introduction of Euro currency.

Like those major business initiatives, e-business forces change to occur to three corporate domains—technology, processes, and people—at both a strategic and an operational (tactical) level.

UNDERTAKING A MAJOR E-BUSINESS EFFORT

Figure 8-1 illustrates where within these domains and levels all of the various issues fall when a company engages in a comprehensive e-business effort.

Figure 8-1   ERP/E-Business Organizational Issues Domain and Level
Matrix

		Technology	Process	People

Impact on Business (High → Low)	Strategic	• Enterprise Architecture
		• Supplier Partnership
		• Role of the Integrator
			• Ownership
			• Design
			• Enterprise-wide
			  (End to End)
				• Change Management
				• Loose/Tight Controls
				• Outsourcing
				• Executive Sponsorship
				  and Support
				• Aligning on Conditions
				  of Satisfaction
				• Overarching Objectives

	Operational	• Product Selection
		• Product Support
		• Implementation/
		  Installations
		• Budgets
			• Change Control
			• Implementation/
			  Support
			• Fluidity
			• Budgets
				• Recruitment
				• Retention
				• Alignment
				• Knowledge Transfer
				• Budgets

Low ——————— Level of Difficulty/Time to Resolve ——————— High

STRATEGIC ISSUES

In a fully developed e-business environment, businesses—and in some cases consumers—will no longer buy simple products from simple companies. They will buy intricately constructed product and service bundles from equally intricately constructed extended enterprises. These will be made up of a fluid set of tightly integrated supply-chain partners, companies that build and manage the network backbone, and a company that owns the customer connection.

Whatever role a company seeks to fill in the e-nabled business world, in order to be ready to participate in an extended enterprise, it will have to show other companies that it has the organizational infrastructure, processes, and human resources, as well as the technology, to be a valuable business partner. Expect that, in the e-nabled world, business partners will measure a company's ability to work with them in all dimensions.

Heightened competition and significantly reduced financial and technological hurdles create the kind of heightened awareness of importance that greatly assists the initial step of change—bringing management on board. The initial challenges on the path to e-business are not insurmountable. Corporate visionaries have the capability to get the ball rolling even within typically change-averse organizations. From that point forward, the barriers are primarily associated with managing change, an area in which great leaders feel challenged but are justified in attacking with fervor. The ability to articulate the compelling reasons to change is essential. Effectively managing change is often overlooked until the project postmortem, at which point change management is usually cited as a key reason for failure and as a problem that could have been easily avoided.

Technology

Strategic technology issues are, for the most part, straightforward and similar to the issues that face any company implementing ERP. An optimal system architecture for any particular enterprise is the first order of the day. Technology should not be allowed to drive the enterprise: rather, technology should fit the enterprise by meeting certain "conditions of satisfaction" with regard to scalability, flexibility, and cost.

A winning technology strategy requires a strong and enduring partnership with key hardware and software suppliers. This drives in-house efficiency and cost effectiveness and also mitigates many risks. Such a strategy could include joint product planning and marketing. A technology integrator, an organization that runs the actual implementation, answers a critical need. This integrator can be an internal project or consulting group; an outside consulting organization; or a hybrid of the two. The integrator's major role is to create consistent output from various inputs (Figure 8-2). The integrator's role extends beyond managing technology to managing process and people issues as well.

Within this role are two major responsibilities. First, the technology integrator synthesizes the enterprise's end-state vision, strategy, and technology architecture with the business-unit drivers. Regardless of whether the company is operated as an "integrated" model with a set of tightly linked business units or as a "holding company" with a set of independently operated business units, the business units must

Figure 8-2   Role of the Integrator: Creating Consistency with an Eye
toward Simplicity

produce e-business connections to the outside world that have a common touch and feel. This is important for brand equity reasons and for
ease of use and effectiveness for customers and suppliers who deal
with more than one business unit for different products or services.

Second, the technology integration establishes an overarching
project plan, including resources and budget requirements, that targets delivery of specific benefits to the business as outlined in the
business case. Again, this is important to do on an enterprise level
regardless of the business-unit operating model. If budgets do not
cover technology requirements, the technology architecture may
need to be changed, harming the effort by possibly suboptimizing the
technical infrastructure.

Options add complexity to creating a program plan in an e-business initiative. Each step down the e-business road contains many
options. But the marketplace is changing more rapidly than ever;

therefore, a company often will have to change direction quickly, abandoning some projects in order to move on to more promising ones. Choosing quickly among options requires flexibility in both program planning and technology. Systems that can "plug and play" with other technologies are easier to adjust quickly.

A technology infrastructure team makes sure that outsiders receive the same touch and feel regardless of which Web front end they click on, and that data being exchanged up and down the supply chain is consistent across applications, business units, and trading partners.

Processes

Engaging effectively in e-business may require engineering new processes or reengineering old ones. Engineering or reengineering end-to-end processes involves identifying all dependencies, key metrics, and resource requirements. Each process must have an enterprise-wide owner, accountable for the process's performance, the budget to execute the process, and the quality of all process deliverables.

If end-to-end processes such as quote-to-cash or design-to-manufacture are to be seen as the customer sees them, organizational boundaries must be dissolved. Subprocess or feeder-process designs establish critical touch points and are often customized "locally." These processes still must be owned by the enterprise and subject to change control, however, to avoid "counterfeit" processes or unauthorized work-arounds.

Operational efforts will move quickly if high-level priorities for operational deployment, by process and/or organizational unit, are established. A well-established and understood process to quickly resolve conflicts is also necessary.

People

Depending on how it is handled, change management will either make or break a company's move to e-business. People can and often do effectively block the success of major technology integration efforts. Not surprisingly, many executives report that their biggest challenge with respect to large technology initiatives is managing change. People barriers remain unchanged—and in some instances are heightened—by the Internet. The ability to manage change is a litmus test for any form of business success. But the change-management challenge in a complex extended enterprise is even greater.

At a strategic level, e-organizations embrace and actively promote the principles of change management embedded in the mnemonic CERTAIN:

Communicate the reason for change.

Enlist the support to change.

Recognize and reward the leaders of change.

Train on the new processes and supporting systems.

Allow for feedback.

Integrate learnings.

Nurture the environment through retraining and reinforcement.

PEOPLE MAKE CHANGE ORGANIC

Living organisms change by leveraging learning and success. Change is elastic and breeds more change, and the more an organization has successfully changed in the past, the more "change friendly" it becomes, having developed a heightened ability to change again and again. Change follows its own laws. The more change occurs upstream, the more it is forced downstream. When leaders change their behaviors as well as their words, that change is driven throughout the organization. But when leaders simply say "you have to change," momentum is not generated upstream.

Marketplace dynamics today are forcing companies to change continuously. But the degree and rate of change must be subtly adjusted by corporate leaders and program managers alike, who must identify those controls that need to be tight and those that need to be loose. Figure 8-3 illustrates these controls, which can continu-

Figure 8-3   Control Points Adjusted Differently

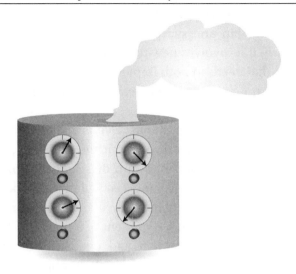

ously be adjusted, as necessary, for both strategic and tactical reasons (for example, slightly loosening the controls on design to provide for uniqueness).

Outsourcing can be an enabler or a disabler, depending on the organization's culture. A company needs to develop a business case for and against outsourcing business processes, systems applications, or the entire e-business effort. Outsourcing requires a clear definition of individual and small-team roles, responsibilities, metrics, and deliverables, both for those who will be maintaining operations and/or for those who will be managing relationships with outsourcing organizations.

EXECUTIVE SPONSORSHIP IS KEY

Strategically, participative executive sponsorship is essential. An executive sponsor reporting directly to the chief operating officer, the president, the chairman, or the office of the chairman leads the change effort. This person is actively involved in offering advice and counsel and in promoting the initiative to executive leadership and across the enterprise. A direct correlation exists between active executive sponsorship and success in any major organizational change, particularly if it involves new technology and new processes. For the company that needs to both implement and continue deploying ERP as part of an e-business initiative, having this kind of sponsorship is even more critical.

The executive sponsor has several major tasks. One is to set appropriate expectations throughout the company, and to periodically communicate progress toward these expectations. Another is to seek support for the remaining tasks, and to work with corporate leadership to eliminate organizational and bureaucratic obstacles. A third is to define and drive alignment of a common set of enterprise-wide conditions of satisfaction and overarching objectives. Senior leaders can use the degree to which these objectives and conditions of satisfaction are being met as the basis for resolving conflicts and rewarding effort.

OPERATIONAL ISSUES

Operational issues revolve around getting e-business initiatives up and running in a timely fashion, adhering to budgets, and maintaining downfield vision so that options can be exercised that are appropriate to the rapid changes in the business and in market conditions.

Technology

Managing the following seven major operational concerns regarding technology is important to any e-business implementation:

1. Develop a product qualification or certification process for the various e-business front-end packages being purchased that ensures product fit, level of performance, and adequate support.
2. Define product support requirements, and establish regularly scheduled product performance review sessions.

3. Define performance expectations, such as system availability, mean time to failure, and mean time to repair.

4. Coordinate the implementation schedule, conduct product training, and monitor performance for product installations.

5. Ensure that operating technology supports the company's business and technology strategy and budget. Web-based technology is comparatively inexpensive, but mistakes can still be costly. In addition, new functionality is being introduced to Web-based technology on almost a weekly basis. There is a high temptation to move to the latest and greatest at a whim, but over the medium to long term, this can wreak havoc with all aspects of the business.

6. Ensure that budget planning, including contingency plans for unexpected conditions, is tightly linked to the release plan. If the technology behind the customer-facing or supplier-facing screen is changed at any time after the Web site and links have gone live, this change must be transparent to the user.

7. Ensure security and data integrity. Effective firewalls placed against the outside world will accomplish this, as will disaster recovery and data backup processes and technology and effective access authorization processes.

Processes

At the operational level, process concerns include meeting the objectives and timelines determined at the strategic level for engineering or reengineering the feeder processes that build up to create the end-to-end processes:

○ An effective change-control mechanism reflects, monitors, and reinforces the operational controls established at the strategy level, and continually "adjusts the knobs" of those controls. Managing an e-business implementation effort must always acknowledge the organic nature of e-business; change occurs as the needs of the business evolve.

- Effective process implementation teams have the authority and ultimate accountability for delivering on process metrics and process benefits.
- Budgets work best when they are tracked on both a process and an organizational basis.

People

At the operational level, managers typically face five major challenges in delivering the key benefits associated with transformational change: organizational scope, change complexity, political resistance, cultural challenge, and change capability. E-business has a significant confounding effect on each one. Plotting a strategy to combat these challenges means recognizing the specific impact of e-business on each issue and to planning accordingly. In addition, the manager of an e-business initiative is also faced with the need to recruit and retain individuals with "hot skills" who may be more inclined to jump to the next exciting opportunity rather than run the ongoing e-business after the implementation. In such an environment, knowledge transfer and knowledge management are the responsibility of each team member and need to be institutionalized.

ORGANIZATIONAL SCOPE

Cross-functional change is particularly difficult. Change across large, complex organizations is even more difficult. Changes across collaborating organizations are perhaps the most difficult of all. E-business, especially where value-chain integration is involved, thrives on the collaboration of partners and customers across geographic, cultural, and business operational divides.

Despite these difficulties, many new entrants have managed to leapfrog into such a collaborative state. The key to their success in these efforts may be the e-nablement of change-management assessment, a process facilitated by Internet communications and applications. Evidence from such diverse operational models as the automobile industry JIT model, Wal-Mart, and Amazon.com suggests that it may actually be easier on a seat-by-seat basis to communicate beyond, rather than within, the company's walls.

CHANGE COMPLEXITY

Complex change is difficult to endure. People's ability to change can be tested beyond its limits. E-business change—the change associated with movement across the e-business panorama—challenges the minds of strategists, not to mention the individuals working in the company's day-to-day operations. Although an outsider might see it as simple, the underlying complexity of intercompany collaboration is daunting. Inability to create a vision of the future breeds uncertainty about the outcomes of an e-business change program. For a company that must implement or reimplement an ERP suite as part of an e-business initiative, change is that much more difficult.

POLITICAL RESISTANCE

Successful change depends on the resolve of leaders at all levels. In the e-business world, knowledge confers power. Multiple power bases and the politics that come with them test leadership resolve, and the extended enterprise only multiplies these effects.

Wherever change creates perceived losers, resistance is high. In the value-chain integration snapshot of the e-business panorama, profits are reallocated throughout the extended enterprise. Whole companies may be subsumed in the process, and others may lose a significant portion of their core business. Gaining commitment from perceived or actual losers will be very difficult, especially when jobs are at risk. Even within the enterprise, the possibility of winners and losers affects the implementation of retention programs. Within an information technology (IT) organization, those who are not working on the hot technology—in this case e-business—may feel unappreciated and less essential in a zero-sum game.

The key to successful e-business implementation, both within a company and within an extended enterprise, is gaining commitment from those who can drive change. All individuals benefit from transparent goals and appropriate rewards for meeting those goals, on both an individual and a team basis.

CULTURAL CHALLENGE

Change is difficult when new ways of working challenge the basic assumptions of a business culture. Cries of "That's not the way we have succeeded up to now" or "Why change now when things are going so well?" ring out during all major change efforts. E-business definitely challenges traditional assumptions in its technology-enabled characteristics, its customer-value-centric view of business, and its reliance on collaboration.

CHANGE CAPABILITY

Organizations that have not succeeded in past change efforts are even less likely to succeed in an e-business implementation because of the challenges it presents to traditional business assumptions. Fostering change may not be possible under existing leadership and management. A company may need to rethink its structure and role in the value network. Some companies may find it easier to break into separate entities, with one being a dot.com, as a method of jump-starting e-business.

The flip side is that companies that have already been successful in managing major change efforts should have an easier time managing implementation of e-business and movement to an extended enterprise environment.

CHANGE-MANAGEMENT APPROACH

The tools of change management, including leadership, communication, training, planning, and incentive systems, can all be used as levers and, when applied correctly, can move great obstacles with a minimum of effort. Conversely, improper application of these levers can have significant negative effects on change initiatives.

Installing technology to make a company ready to become an effective member of an extended enterprise is easy. The difficulty lies in preparing the company organizationally. Successful change managers recognize the complexity of the challenge and adopt a structured approach to applying the tools that facilitate rapid change. Figure 8-4 illustrates the steps that a company can take to show potential partners that the company is ready, willing, and able to do business in an e-nabled world.

Create a Change Vision

A vision of change must be a coherent and powerful statement of what the company seeks to do in the e-nabled world, what place it will play in an extended enterprise, and what skills and competencies it brings to the extended organization. A clear and concise corporate vision in the e-business world and elsewhere challenges the company to move outside its comfort zone to take risks. It motivates and inspires employees by reducing ambiguity and by involving them in leadership's view of the future. A vision aligns diverse organizational elements within the company toward a common goal.

A vision is especially important as it pertains to merging the mandate of the IT department, which controls—in some cases by default—the company's ERP system; and to the various supply-facing and demand-facing organizational elements that are focused on enhancing their operations through use of Web-based technology.

Define Change Strategy

Developing a change strategy is an iterative process involving assessment, strategy formulation, planning, and determining roles and governance. The process is often repeated two or three times in a change life cycle, each time in increasing detail. When the change involves implementation of ERP, this reiteration helps sharpen the

Figure 8-4   Eight-Step Change Process

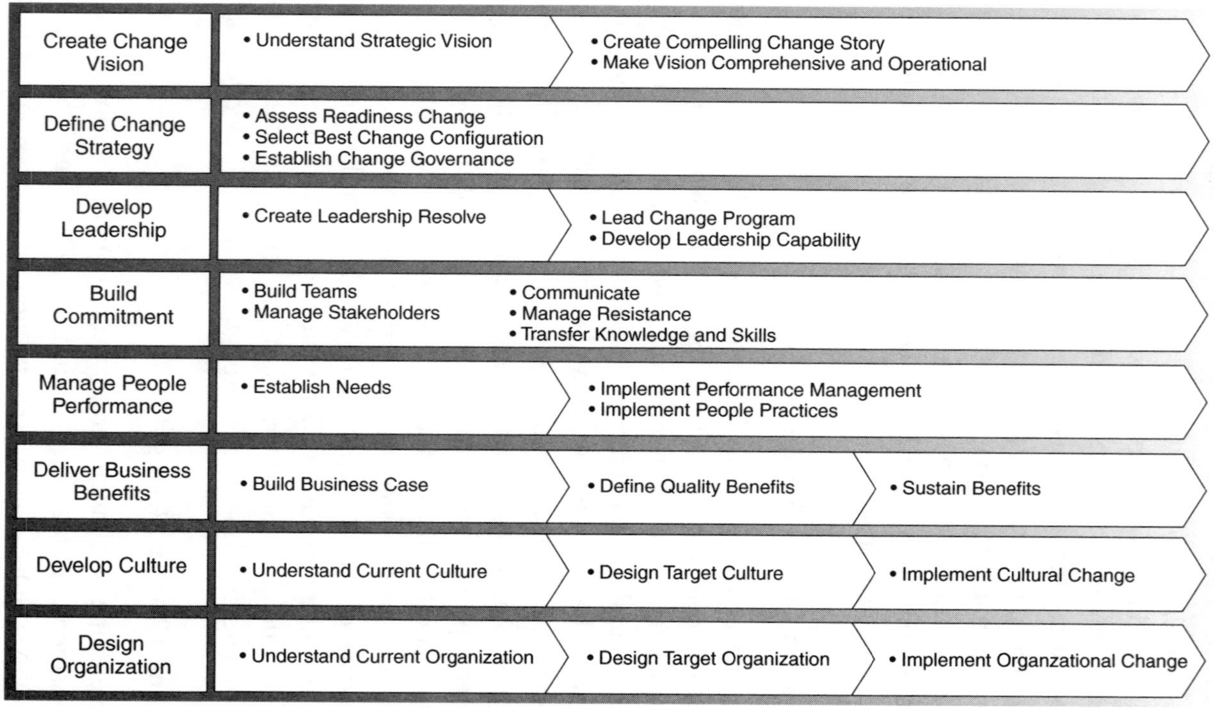

Create Change Vision	• Understand Strategic Vision	• Create Compelling Change Story • Make Vision Comprehensive and Operational
Define Change Strategy	• Assess Readiness Change • Select Best Change Configuration • Establish Change Governance	
Develop Leadership	• Create Leadership Resolve	• Lead Change Program • Develop Leadership Capability
Build Commitment	• Build Teams • Manage Stakeholders	• Communicate • Manage Resistance • Transfer Knowledge and Skills
Manage People Performance	• Establish Needs	• Implement Performance Management • Implement People Practices
Deliver Business Benefits	• Build Business Case	• Define Quality Benefits · Sustain Benefits
Develop Culture	• Understand Current Culture	• Design Target Culture · Implement Cultural Change
Design Organization	• Understand Current Organization	• Design Target Organization · Implement Organizational Change

focus of the effort and reenergize the organization. In the e-business world, there may be less opportunity to refine the change strategy within each project because of the speed at which each is undertaken. More effort, however, should be made to revisit the change strategy between e-business projects to make subsequent efforts more effective.

Develop Change Leadership

Change leadership is at the center of successful change. Surveys often find that program leadership is in place before the initiative begins in about one quarter of major change efforts. Change leadership is not the same as project leadership. Confusing the two distinct roles often leads to failure. Change leaders are change agents, concerned with the holistic elements of change and not the day-to-day activities that are changing. Successful change requires a clear contract between project leadership and the change leader.

Change leadership must be different for an e-business undertaking than for an ERP implementation in which e-business is not involved. Whereas that kind of ERP change is primarily internal to the organization, the e-business component involves drastically changing relationships with customers, suppliers, and business partners, all of whom must be considered and informed during the change effort.

Build Commitment to Change

Change can be achieved through commitment or compliance. Building commitment, usually the goal of change, is expensive. Companies should not pay for more commitment than they actually need. The constraints on a company seeking to be an extended enterprise leader include lack of control over potential business partner organizations. Thus, while it may be possible to achieve change internally through compliance tactics, extended enterprise-level e-business change requires commitment on the part of customers, suppliers, and business partners.

Fortunately, Web-based technology provides unique methods of executing communication plans and gaining commitment. In the same way that companies use tools that facilitate a "market of one," they can target change-management communications to an "audience of one." Figure 8-5 compares some compliance tactics that can be used internally with some commitment tactics that can be used across an extended enterprise.

Manage People and Performance

Performance management is about controlling behavior through measured performance. A company's goals should be linked to the performance metrics it uses to motivate actions. In the best case, highly transparent goals communicate the changes in activities

Figure 8-5   Change Tactics

Internal Compliance Tactics	Extended Enterprise-wide Commitment Tactics
• Change Information Systems • Reduce Headcount • Change Organizational Structure • New Meeting Structure • New Workplace Design • New Administration Process • Change Sign-Off Process	• Build Teams - Project Teams - Work Group Teams • Manage Stakeholders - Understand Needs - Face-to-Face Meetings • Communicate Change - With Stakeholders - With Project Teams • Transfer Knowledge and Skills - New Ways of Working - Change Skills • Manage Resistance - Understand Causes - Engage Resisters - Resolve Conflicts • Drive Alignment

employees are required to make throughout the organization, in a single company or in an extended enterprise.

Performance measures that are easily understood are readily accepted by those whose performance will be measured by them. A cascading system in which a manager is measured by his or her team's performance enhances acceptance. The reward system must be tightly linked to attainment of metrics.

Define Business Benefits

The challenge of sustained business benefit delivery is considerable. A successful change effort requires not only development of a value proposition and business case, but also a definition of how benefits will be quantified throughout the project's life. Terms of reference that make clear the business case and set direction so all participants are clear about what they must deliver, when, and at what cost and risk are important.

Benefits attached to project milestones in the plan make clear what will be delivered, by whom, and when. A change-load assessment establishes whether an organization's process can assimilate these changes. A change-load assessment process that identifies temporal overlaps in change requirements and shows the need to make tough choices about the timing and level of planned change is important to the overall change strategy.

Develop Culture

Culture is the combination of values and beliefs that provide direction and energy to what people do each day. It is visible throughout a company in artifacts and manifestations such as performance standards, icons, myths and stories, rituals, traditions, language, and relationships. Cultural values and beliefs are deeply seated and affect individual and organizational behavior every day. For example, they influence the way people are rewarded or the way they are encouraged to seek forgiveness or ask permission before taking risks. Behaviors need to match market needs and be capable of evolving as these needs change.

135

Education, in contrast to training, is the key delivery method for imparting cultural change. As a company becomes an e-business, it will still run a portion of its day-to-day operations in a non–e-nabled way. Yet, because e-business will, over time, change the fundamental business model of so many companies, every employee must be educated about e-business. This is a major change from non–e-business-related ERP, where training was delivered just to those who needed to use the system.

Design Organization

The final step in undertaking radical change is designing an organization that encompasses the new way of doing business. Organizational design is crucial for companies facing e-business challenges. Organizational design elements include the reporting structure, roles, performance measures, work groups, and integrating mechanisms. E-business-related challenges include changing global economic factors: work force expectations and regulatory environments, more demanding customers, a globalizing marketplace, global competition, and the continuing emergence of new technology.

In the change involved in ERP implementation, a company has to address two vital organizational design issues: enterprise-wide (corporate center and business unit) design, and unit-level (work unit and individual position) design. When engaging in change around e-business, however, a company has to add a third level of complexity: the design issues facing the extended enterprise value chain or even value chains that today seem totally different but that will ultimately converge.

9

ERP/E-Business Matrix Destination Goals

The two large truths about e-business are:

1. E-business is about strategy; it is not about technology.
2. E-business is about speed and flexibility; achieving speed and flexibility requires maintaining as many options as possible.

Large, global companies confronting e-business determine how to change their business model to accomodate new realities while maintaining and capitalizing on all that they already do well. One of the things many large companies do increasingly well is manage their internal information flows using ERP technology.

SIX REGIONS ON THE ERP/E-BUSINESS MATRIX DEFINED

Our premise throughout this book is that e-business and ERP technologies work hand in hand, each one supercharging the other and, ultimately, merging into a single, seamless solution. For the present, however, it is still possible to define segments of the ERP/e-business matrix and the positive and negative aspects of a company occupying any one of those regions. The 25-box ERP/e-business matrix (Figure 9-1) contains six regions.

For twenty-first-century companies, these bounded regions suggest two questions: (1) Why might I want to go there? and (2) How might I get there from where I am now? This chapter will focus on the first question.

Where Might a Company Go and Why?

Region I (start-up) represents the opening position for a new dot.com company entering the business world today. A company does not choose to be in this region; rather, it lands there by default. It is at the beginning of its life and moves out of this region very quickly. The company must decide whether to focus its energy on moving left to right across the e-business landscape as quickly as

Figure 9-1   ERP/E-Business Organizational Issues: Domain and Level Matrix

	No E-Business Capabilities	Channel Enhancement	Value-Chain Integration	Industry Transformation	Convergence
Greenfield	I. Start-Up		II. Enterprise Growth Limited (High Risk = Opportunity)		
Nonintegrated Systems			IV. High Cost Relative to Benefit		
Limited/Single-Function ERP	III. Customer Benefit Limited				
Integrated Business-Unit ERP	Reduced E-Options and Flexibility		V. Optimize Business at Unit Level		
Integrated Enterprise ERP			VI. Optimize across Enterprise		

possible, implementing an ERP system, or dividing its energy and moving to an ERP infrastructure as it simultaneously journeys across the e-business landscape. This decision would be based largely on the competitive landscape, business partnerships, and internal capabilities.

Region II (Enterprise Growth Limited [High Risk=Opportunity]) is a continuation along the greenfield ERP axis. For a new company, this is a possible option. The company has significant technological skills and assumes it can continue to grow without implementing ERP. Upside attributes of being in this region include the following: The company does not have to put time, money, and human resources into installing ERP technology, and can take advantage of the full flexibility of best-in-class Web-based technology without having to worry about what front-end technology will work with its ERP system. The downside is that lack of a supporting technological infrastructure limits the internal organizational complexity and scale it can develop, potentially resulting in limited growth, unless and until a technological breakthrough occurs that supersedes ERP systems. In this region, although e-business front ends might be sophisticated, internal processes might be manual or desktop-oriented, with little or no integration, making partnering difficult. In the future, if vendors of front-end Web-based technology beef up their transaction-processing engines, if ERP vendors or others develop "ERP light" solutions, a company in this position could take advantage of one of those options.

Region III (Customer Benefit Limited, Reduced E-Options and Flexibility) includes eight boxes, bounded by the four other ERP-axis environments and the first two boxes along the e-business panorama. This region has few if any positive attributes. Customer benefits are limited, and there is little flexibility to move further along the e-business landscape. If a company merely opens an e-commerce channel, it is behind the e-business curve and will very shortly find that it cannot satisfy customer and supplier needs. If a company finds itself in this region, it should seek to leave it as soon as possible so that it can either improve its internal business processes or become further e-nabled. In this region, internal manual systems limit the company's ability to grow, and lack of integrated company information limits its ability to partner with other companies.

Companies that have integrated ERP technology, either at the business-unit level or across the enterprise, should seek to move directly to the right along the e-business panorama. Companies that have either nonintegrated legacy systems or limited single-function ERP need to decide how much of their resources to put into moving along the e-business panorama and how much they need to put into developing a more fully integrated ERP system. Deciding whether to integrate at the business-unit level or across the enterprise depends on how the company is organized. If the business units are stand-alone companies, producing different goods and services, and the company is managed as a holding company, ERP can be integrated by business unit. If the business units are part of the same value chain, then the company should move to integrate at the enterprise level.

Two of the boxes in this region—Integrated Business-Unit ERP/Channel Enhancement and Integrated Enterprise ERP/Channel Enhancement—make up a subregion that is a legitimate starting point for companies with integrated ERP technology. To reside in this region, it is necessary to have an e-commerce channel and to use this snapshot on the e-business landscape as a learning opportunity before moving into more complex e-business constructs.

Region IV on the matrix (High Cost Relative to Benefit) comprises six boxes, along two ERP axes and across three e-business snapshots. In this region, a high level of effort is needed to gather data, process transactions, and improve technology. Timelines here are long and there are multiple system interfaces. And, if e-business efforts are successful, human capacity becomes pushed to the limit as the infrastructure is overwhelmed by orders coming through the e-business front end. Already, some manufacturing companies and dot.com retailers have been brought to their knees by the flood of e-business orders coming into nonintegrated manufacturing and distribution systems.

Except for a pure information company—some sort of infomediary—once a company wants to integrate with value-chain business partners and create an extended enterprise that changes the basis of competition in an industry, it must have the ability to manage internal information flows via ERP. To date, there is no transaction- and information-processing engine powerful enough to perform these tasks except ERP.

Region V (Optimize Business at Unit Level) is the integrated business-unit ERP axis across value-chain integration, industry transformation, and convergence. Region VI (Optimize across Enterprise) is the integrated enterprise ERP axis across the same e-business snapshots. As Figure 9-2 illustrates, most companies will want to be in either of these two regions as quickly as possible.

Figure 9-2   Possible Destinations

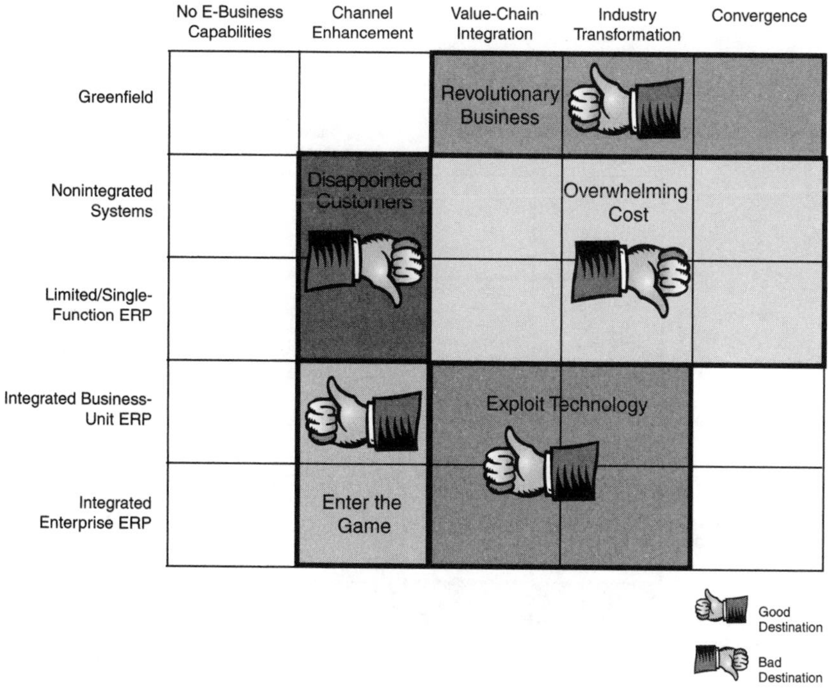

Starting Point: Where Are Most Companies Now?

Today, most companies find themselves in one of the six boxes shown in Figure 9-3. Shaded boxes contain the various e-possibilities and e-characteristics.

The majority of companies, in fact, are in some way involved with the Internet. However, many have found it difficult to develop Internet-selling capabilities, and continue to use their Web sites as "brochureware." Such companies, however, do have the capability to work with business partners through proprietary electronic data interchange (EDI) technology. For those with ERP, either by business unit or by function, such EDI capabilities are less resource-consuming than for companies with nonintegrated systems.

Cutting-edge companies have moved into value-chain integration, at least tentatively, with their business partners up and down the value chain. Just now, the first extended enterprises are beginning to appear and transform industries. Infomediaries are also transforming

Figure 9-3   Where Most Companies Are Now

	No E-Business Capabilities	Channel Enhancement	Value-Chain Integration	Industry Transformation	Convergence
Greenfield					
Nonintegrated Systems	EDI possible, but inflexible and expensive	Front-end Web site to single system			
Limited/Single-Function ERP	EDI possible, streamlining functions possible	Front-end Web site to single function			
Integrated Business-Unit ERP	EDI possible, streamlining single business-unit processes possible	On-line Unit Catalog Order status tracking Corp Web site			
Integrated Enterprise ERP					

industries and changing the roles that physical goods–producing companies play in various industries.

Convergence, in industries in which it is occurring, is usually being driven by other considerations, such as deregulation. The telecommunications industry is a good example of this. Telco providers are consolidating (MCI/WorldCom, Vodaphone/Mannesman, AT&T/TCI) due to deregulation and privatization. This trend is being accelerated by Internet telephony, mobile computing, broad band access, and lower costs for all these technologies. The ability of telco companies to flourish will be based on their flexibility, speed, and partnering capability.

End Point: Where Most Companies Ought to Be

In order to take full advantage of e-business opportunities, companies will need ERP technology, integrated at either the business-unit or enterprise level (Figure 9-4.) Again, the shaded boxes contain the e-possibilities and the e-characteristics.

Figure 9-4   Where Most Companies Are Headed

	No E-Business Capabilities	Channel Enhancement	Value-Chain Integration	Industry Transformation	Convergence
Greenfield					
Nonintegrated Systems					
Limited/Single-Function ERP					
Integrated Business-Unit ERP		On-line unit catalog Order status tracking Corp Web site	Partnering within enterprise Unit e-partnering outside Outsource unit by unit	Unit-led e-consortiums etc., but no enterprise-level synergies	
Integrated Enterprise ERP		Product configuration On-line Enterprise Catalog Order status tracking Corp Web site	Re/disintermediation E-partnering Full business process outsourcing	Industry reengineering Virtual organization E-consortiums	

Companies that do not have true e-commerce channels that allow for Web-based sales, and product configurations when appropriate, may not be in business very long; if they are, they will certainly struggle to explain their plans to their customers, suppliers, and business partners. Most companies will have engaged in significant value-chain integration, either as the company driving the integration or as a supplier feeding into a number of extended enterprises driven by other companies.

Extended enterprises will continue to develop, and they will transform many industries. The ability of extended enterprises to use their competencies to cross industries will enhance the movement toward convergence. These enterprises will take advantage of increased deregulation and globalization.

GETTING FROM HERE TO THERE

The migration path any particular company might take to get from its starting point to a successful end point varies. Regardless of the particular migration path a company decides to take, it will need to meet nine conditions to be successful:

1. Senior executive support
2. Change linked to business strategy
3. Supportive staff
4. Proactive teams
5. Software and hardware integration
6. Defined and refined business processes
7. Data integrity
8. Wisely chosen business partners
9. Ability to innovate.

Senior Executive Support

A committed senior executive is one of the most important factors in successful change. This leader must have time, capability, authority, and credibility. He or she must be able to muster the necessary organizational resources, to facilitate decision making, and to communicate at all levels of the enterprise or business unit about the importance of both ERP and e-business.

Change Linked to Business Strategy

The enterprise or business-unit leaders must view the benefits of moving into the e-business world and cement e-business capabilities with ERP technology at a strategic level. Leaders must expect competitive advantage to be gained from the changes and understand how it will be measured. E-business and ERP must also be linked closely to the company's tactical goals, such as integrating value chains and developing shared services capabilities.

Supportive Staff

To succeed in the e-world, a positive attitude to change is necessary. This attitude can be created through training and persuasion, and through honest communication. However, the largest factor in successful change is a history of having done it before. Companies that have already successfully implemented ERP at a business unit or throughout the enterprise will have a leg up on those companies trying to implement e-business and ERP simultaneously. Companies that have successfully undergone business process reengineering (BPR) and/or successfully implemented shared service centers for nonstrategic business processes are also well positioned for success. A culture adaptive to change, and a staff with the necessary skills to manage change, are the best tools to ensure success.

Proactive Teams

Any ERP or e-business design and/or implementation team must have on it a number of people who are knowledgeable of both the company's business and the new technology. Enthusiasm, good communication skills, and the willingness to work with other people to find creative solutions are also essential qualities for team members.

Software and Hardware Integration

Software facilitates the integration of data, and hardware must be open to allow seamless cross-platform communication. Any company looking to integrate ERP and Web-based technologies must capitalize on the most relevant technological advances.

Defined and Refined Business Processes

There must be agreement on the way of doing business within the business unit or enterprise and across enterprises. Companies within an extended enterprise that have already undergone BPR to wring out inefficiencies and increase effectiveness should share their knowledge with other extended enterprise members in order to create the most efficient and effective extraprise processes. Essentially, value networks must agree on how they will conduct their business on the Internet.

Data Standards and Integrity

Data standards are essential. Whenever possible, open standards are preferable. Companies must establish the language of data exchange (Extensible Markup Language, Internet Protocol), as well as the words (data dictionaries) and dialogue (process and workflow). Without establishing these standards, no electronic exchange of business information (that is, no e-nabled business partnerships) can take place. Once the standards are established, all business partners must provide data that is clean, consistent, and reliable, both within each business unit or enterprise and across enterprises within an extraprise.

Wisely Chosen Business Partners

Every business partner within an extended enterprise must be chosen with the above characteristics in mind. In the extended enterprise, the slowest partner sets the speed of business. The first step in partnering with any business in this manner is a thorough assessment of its capabilities. If the company does not measure up, it does not belong in the enterprise or it should be brought up to standards. All business partners should take the same critical look at each other.

Ability to Innovate

Innovation is the core of a company's ability to adopt new business practices dynamically, to thrive on new technologies, and to become (and remain) leaders in industry and market segments. Innovative thinking leads to daily breakthroughs at all levels, which are necessary for a company to change quickly enough to stay ahead of the competition. A company's ability to innovate continually is cultural, requires management support, and is based on a willingness to try new things and accept that some of them will fail.

10

Migration Path Options

Most companies recognize the importance of becoming e-nabled. In fact, most have already started working in this regard. For many companies, however, the work to date has not been part of a systematic and focused approach that will result in the enterprise's getting maximum benefit in the shortest amount of time. Instead, these companies take a haphazard approach to e-business development, with disconnected project teams, disjointed technological investments, and unclear strategic objectives. Consequently, they must find a way to streamline the planning process relative to e-business strategy.

Many companies' efforts at e-business often result in confusion and disappointment for customers, suppliers, and employees. The ERP/e-business matrix and the migration paths described in this chapter allow a company to make some sense of its options. Four steps are required to undertake an appropriate migration from any starting point on the ERP/e-business matrix to one of the preferred destination points, which are bounded by Integrated Business-Unit ERP or Integrated Enterprise ERP on the ERP axis, and by value-chain integration or industry transformation on the e-business axis:

1. Determine where the company is going and why.
2. Assess organizational capabilities to get there in the most expeditious way.

3. Plan the route forward.

4. Implement on the route forward.

DETERMINE WHERE THE COMPANY IS GOING AND WHY

The e-business panorama model highlights new business possibilities. E-business, first and foremost, provides new strategic options, including collaborating with customers and suppliers in new ways, as well as new internal business models. In order to determine which opportunities make the most sense, a company needs to assess its core competencies and key business processes. Then it must determine how Web-based technology can be used to enhance processes; to most efficiently bring competencies in from outside business partners; and to leverage on behalf of those partners the company's strong capabilities.

Collaboration with customers and suppliers can have the most immediate impact on planning and forecasting, order entry and tracking, product design and configuration, or order settlement, although plenty of other options are possible, based on the specifics of the business partnership and the industry. Internal business-model changes can include development or reinvigoration of shared service centers, setup and distribution of software, and cost-reduction opportunities. E-business may also be the way business units within an enterprise integrate more tightly—intra-enterprise integration that allows business units to act as better business partners.

Each of these areas will surely offer more opportunities as time goes on, demanding a consistent reassessment of e-business options as the business environment and technologies constantly evolve. Once this has been accomplished, the company can establish a vision and a business case for e-business. The vision might include one or more of the following priorities:

○ Building customer loyalty
○ Achieving market leadership

o Streamlining and extending processes

o Creating new products and services

o Penetrating new markets

o Reducing costs.

Such a vision is developed at the company level, regardless of the business-unit model (integrated business units that make up an enterprise or independently operated business units operated in a holding company model) under which the company operates. The vision should be driven from the enterprise to the business units, rather than the other way around. The key point is that the approach to developing a business strategy that properly considers e-business transformation is really no different than developing a strategy without e-business. The only difference is the potential strategic options, and a more sophisticated approach to evaluating them, such as real options valuation (ROV™). (See Chapter 3.)

In a decentralized model, the enterprise vision might be somewhat general, but it will at least give business-unit leaders both a direction and parameters within which to work. This is important if the company's e-business efforts are to present "one face to the customer" and maintain brand image. From this vision comes a strategy, and from the strategy come the individual e-business projects within the business units and/or the enterprise. The strategy itself needs a business case, which can be developed using both discounted cash flow (DCF) and ROV™ techniques.

ASSESS ORGANIZATIONAL CAPABILITIES
TO GET THERE

Once a company knows where it is starting from and where it wants to go, it needs to assess its ability to get there. This means assessing its organizational capabilities in the three variables discussed in Chapter 8; technology, processes, and people. To be workable, a migration path must be chosen realistically, based on true delivery capabilities of these three key dimensions that most critically affect the success of any corporate change effort.

In the area of technology, a company needs to assess its current ERP software and existing Web-based technology, as well as any other packaged software, homegrown software, and electronic data interchange (EDI) technology. It is important to understand the ERP system's e-business capabilities at the time of the assessment, as well as its potential.

Additionally, the company needs to assess its data standards. How is data handled inside the enterprise? Do all systems use common coding? Are translations between data formats clearly defined? Is middleware in place that handles transfers between systems in a standard manner? Is messaging performed in a common way between systems?

The purpose of assessing the technology is to establish an overall technology migration architecture that defines the path from today's technology to tomorrow's, at the enterprise level. In the area of business processes, the company needs to assess the current efficiency and effectiveness of each process to identify those processes that are critical to the enterprise in both the short and long term. The company can then determine which processes it wants to maintain at all costs, which it wants to outsource in an arm's-length contractor relationship, and which it would consider letting a business partner take over as part of an extended enterprise.

With regard to people, the company should measure the capacity of its people to deal with change. Have they succeeded in integrating prior changes? Have they overcome the natural tendency to resist change? Are they ready for yet another change, or are they burned out from constant major change efforts over the last five or ten years? Conducting a change-readiness survey on a representative population and applying appropriate change-management techniques early in the change process can be useful.

In addition to assessing its own capabilities, the company should assess these capabilities among potential business partners throughout the value chain. It should also evaluate each partner's or potential partner's technical capabilities, processes, organizational characteristics, and executive commitment to working in an extended enterprise, and determine how easy or difficult it is to standardize partner data against company data to ensure the possibility of electronic communication.

PLAN THE ROUTE FORWARD

To determine a way forward, companies must achieve a realistic balance among organizational change capabilities, technological options, and business partner interests, resulting in the enterprise's meeting its strategic objectives. A good place to start is with a review of the various software options for getting the ERP system (if there is one) Web compatible. These might include ERP provider Web front ends, front ends that work best with the ERP system, or best-in-class Web front ends that can be integrated with the ERP.

The company must choose a path that meets the strategic needs of the enterprise or business unit, and e-nables all of the enterprise's or business unit's core processes. This path must capitalize on the enterprise's or business unit's strengths and be achievable. The technology changeover must be possible. Staff must be willing and able to move along the path. Leadership must promote the chosen path, and the path must be affordable.

A successful migration path is made possible by building a realistic set of clear and manageable projects of reasonable size, all of which are harmonious and move toward a common goal. In short, the migration must get a company to its ultimate goal by way of a series of steps that can be accomplished within the constraints of the organization's competencies.

To do this, a company must choose to employ one of four general approaches moving forward:

1. Bet on the realistic unknown.
   o A company can bet that a realistic—but at this time unknown—technology and/or way of working will evolve

over the next few years that allows the company to run its operations using some non-ERP technology. This is a possible but unlikely scenario.

- The above approach is appropriate only for start-up Internet-focused companies that have no legacy business processes or computer systems because they are best positioned to work and operate successfully in radical new ways.

2. Get the company's house in order.

- Under this approach, a company should clean up internal data, align internal processes to consistently support business objectives, and establish a track record of successful change before entering the e-business environment in a big way. Such a company wants to learn new technologies and exploit shared services. A company adopting this approach will move in small, incremental steps, and may wish to get to the ERP axis it wants to be on before moving too far along the e-business panorama.

- A company taking this approach recognizes that jumping into the e-business fray without being fully ready with aligned internal processes and integrated computer systems is not the best way to succeed. In fact, in the e-business environment, making empty promises to customers and business partners could be worse than delaying entry.

3. Stretch.

- A company following a stretch approach will want to move across the e-business panorama and down the ERP axes simultaneously. An enterprise or business unit can embrace this approach if it has a track record of successfully integrating major change efforts, if leadership is used to and willing to drive change forward to deliver strategic goals, and if there is a critical mass of people who truly understand Web-based technology. We believe this approach can be risky and should be taken only if the company is confident that it can manage change.

4. Exploit across the business unit or enterprise.

   o This approach is really open only to companies that have implemented integrated ERP, either at the business-unit or enterprise level, and that are comfortable with that level of integration. Such a company can move rapidly across the e-business panorama since it does not have to put any resources into an ERP effort.

The key is to develop a plan that balances cost, benefits, and risks. A company that attempts to take on too much too soon will ultimately fail or severely strain customer and partner relationships.

Key Questions to Ask Regarding Any Migration Path

When implementing a migration path utilizing any of these approaches, corporate leadership needs to ask a series of questions:

1. How do I know when I'm getting enough out of the route I have taken? When should I consider alternative paths?

   o This point will come when key factors change, such as organizational acceptance of change, technological capabilities, or business partner capabilities.

2. How do I weight the business case for integrating ERP first against the business case for implementing some e-business first?

   o The answer to this is embedded within the overall business strategy, which establishes business priorities. A company should not be implementing technology without a clear strategic need.

3. Is it always faster to stretch diagonally across the e-business panorama and down the ERP axis simultaneously, or might it be quicker in some instances to move horizontally and then vertically, or vertically and then horizontally?

○ The answer is different for each company because it is based on the company's organizational capability to adapt and change.

4. How do I determine if my company has enough organizational horsepower to stretch?

○ An objective review of the company's track record for managing large change initiatives will provide the insight necessary to answer this question. Also, there are a number of organizational readiness assessment tools that can be administered.

IMPLEMENT ON THE ROUTE FORWARD

On the route forward across the e-business panorama, a company might legitimately stop at any point, consolidate its efforts before moving on, and possibly even decide not to move any further. For each of the five ERP starting points, a company will go through a number of decision points. The entire migration path does not have to be mapped out at the beginning of the journey; in fact, business-unit or enterprise leaders should remain open-minded and flexible about possibly changing either their end goal or their route to get there. A migration path strategy should be redefined every three-to-six months, as business conditions in a particular industry warrant.

Greenfield

A company on the greenfield ERP axis has a number of possible options. Figure 10-1 illustrates all of these possibilities. The company can decide not to implement ERP and seek to move across the e-business panorama as quickly as possible, hoping that technology will become available to allow it to process transactions and manage internal information without the need for ERP technology. It can also seek to implement ERP and e-business simultaneously, moving from its starting point to either an integrated business unit or integrated enterprise ERP at the same time it moves one, two, or even three snapshots across the e-business landscape.

Figure 10-1   Greenfield ERP Migration Options

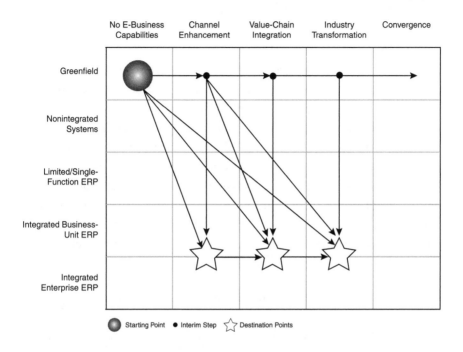

Going from the starting point to ERP integration in the channel enhancement snapshot is "going for channel," because the prime objective is to establish a strong presence on this basis. Moving from the starting point to ERP integration in the value-chain integration stage is "going for the unique business model," because of the many possibilities that exist for a company in this space today. Moving from the starting point to ERP integration in the industry transformation stage is "going for industry leadership," because of the immense potential of this approach.

A company starting from scratch can also move to a particular step along the e-business panorama and then make the decision to install integrated ERP at either the business-unit or enterprise level, either as a next step or simultaneously while moving to the next stage along the e-business panorama. A company starting fresh would very rarely, if ever, implement an integrated ERP system prior to moving along the e-business landscape.

Nonintegrated Systems

The company starting with nonintegrated internal systems has many of the same options as the greenfield company but is constrained by its starting position. Figure 10-2 illustrates a map of possible migration paths for such a company. Such a company can seek to get its house in order and implement ERP, either by business unit or enterprise, before beginning its e-business journey. Or it can develop some e-business skills first and then move to implement ERP. Such a company cannot move too far across the e-business landscape before it becomes necessary to implement ERP. Somewhere in the value-chain integration snapshot, it should become apparent to such a com-

Figure 10-2   Nonintegrated Systems Migration Options

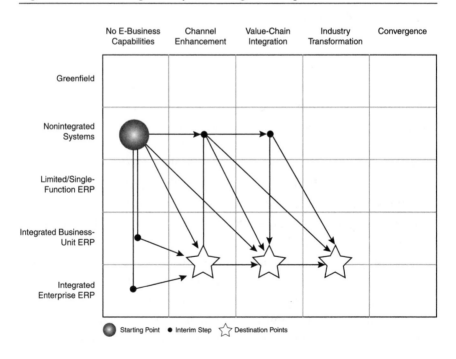

pany that in order to be most efficient and effective, it needs to have better control of its internal information. Such a company, in fact, may be forced to implement ERP by a stronger partner in the developing value network.

At any stage along the e-business landscape, the nonintegrated company can decide either to implement ERP before moving on to the next snapshot or to stretch its efforts and implement ERP while simultaneously moving to the next snapshot in the panorama.

Limited/Single-Function ERP

A company starting with limited/single-function ERP has a set of migration path options similar to the company with nonintegrated systems. These are illustrated in Figure 10-3. The company can get its house in order and integrate its ERP across business units or the enterprise and then develop e-business skills, or it can develop e-busi-

Figure 10-3   Limited/Single-Function ERP Migration Options

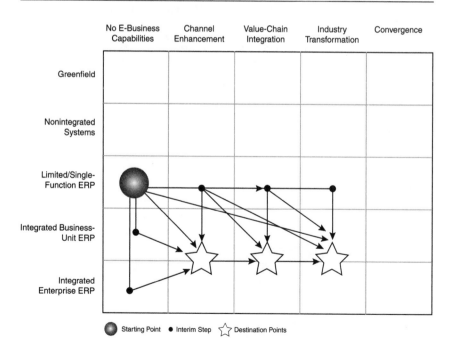

ness skills first. Such a company would find it easier than the nonintegrated company to implement integrated ERP, since it has dealt, at least in part, with the change issues involved in moving to an ERP system. If the company decides to gain e-business skills first, it can stop at any snapshot on the e-business panorama and then implement an integrated ERP system before moving on in the e-business world, or it can stretch its efforts and implement an integrated ERP system at the same time that it moves across snapshots in the e-business panorama.

Integrated Business-Unit ERP

A company that has already integrated ERP across business units has a small constellation of migration paths (Figure 10-4). The first issue is whether the company remains comfortable having its ERP integrated by business units, or whether it feels that in the e-business world it

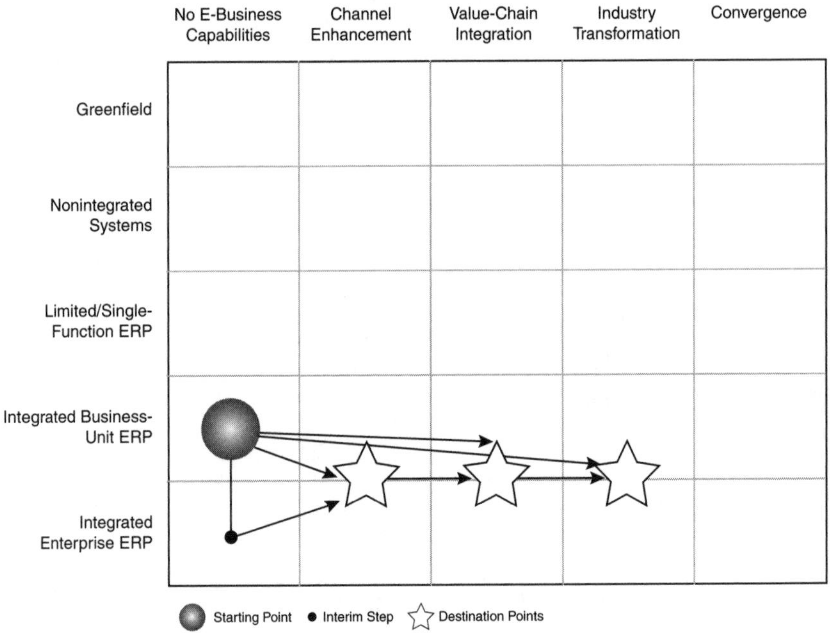

Figure 10-4   Integrated Business-Unit ERP Migration Options

would be more advantageous to be integrated across the enterprise. If such a company feels comfortable remaining integrated by business unit, it can exploit its integration and move consistently across the e-business panorama, or it can seek to stretch by immediately moving into value-chain integration or industry transformation. If such a company feels it must integrate at the enterprise level, it can either perform that integration immediately, then move across the e-business panorama, or it can integrate at the enterprise level while simultaneously moving to the e-commerce channel or simultaneously stretching to value-chain integration or industry transformation.

Integrated Enterprise ERP

The company that has ERP integrated across the enterprise has a number of migration path options (Figure 10-5). Such a company can either move consistently across the e-business panorama or stretch

Figure 10-5   Integrated Enterprise ERP Migration Options

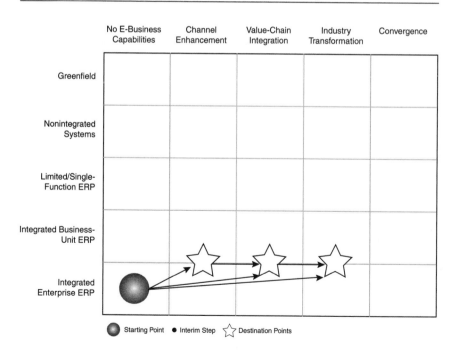

across two or three snapshots into value-chain integration or industry transformation. In all cases, a company must determine a path forward that meets its strategic objectives within a reasonable time frame and at an acceptable cost. This involves carefully balancing organizational capabilities with technological possibilities and business partner interests.

Each company's situation will be unique. But e-business efforts must be managed in a systematic manner, as befits any strategic initiative. Specifically, this means that these efforts must be controlled at a senior leadership level and coordinated appropriately across the enterprise. Web-based technology has pushed information technology questions even higher up the corporate ladder. Senior executives must now become even more familiar with and engaged in technology to make their companies successful.

11

Program and Project Management

Working with hundreds of ERP installations during the 1990s, we found that top-notch project and program management is one of the key prerequisites for success. This is also true for companies' undertaking major e-business initiatives. However, because of the differences in the nature of ERP and e-business undertakings, the duties of both program and project managers also will be different.

PROGRAM MANAGEMENT

For either an ERP installation or an e-business effort, the program is the collection of individual projects, and the job of the program manager is to make sure that all the various projects are carried out in the appropriate sequence and are on time and on budget. Program management, however, differs for the two types of efforts. In an ERP installation, the individual projects are intimately related to one another; in an e-business effort, the projects are more a group of discrete point solutions. Usually, more e-business projects go on at any one time than projects in an ERP installation. Whereas the projects in an ERP installation generally finish up in one "go-live" time frame or a series of linked, coordinated, and interdependent go-lives, e-business projects get up and running as they are ready.

In either an ERP installation or an e-business effort, the keys to program management are alignment and balance. Program managers must align the objectives of each individual project with the company's overall strategy, approach, and direction. They seek to balance the resources going to individual projects to keep all projects on track. Program managers are also responsible for mediating and resolving conflicts as different projects jostle for resources.

Program managers are most concerned about one central issue: Can teams achieve their milestones within acceptable time frames? To answer this question, program managers must look at whether each team has the resources necessary to succeed. The program manager is responsible for allocating often scarce internal business and technical resources, as well as any consulting resources, across the spectrum of projects. Only when resources are allocated appropriately can each team be expected to achieve its deliverables.

In any project, however, success is assured if:

- Stakeholders are committed.
- Business benefits are realized.
- Work and schedule are predictable.
- The team is high performing.
- The scope is realistic and managed.
- Risks are mitigated.
- Delivery organization benefits are realized.

BUSINESS MODEL AND GOVERNANCE STRUCTURE

The way the company is organized—as a collection of independently operated business units within a "holding company" or as interdependent business units within a tightly integrated enterprise—has an influence on how the program management operates. In a centralized company, in which there is corporate control over all business units, the program manager usually has a lot of control over budgets and resources. In a decentralized company, the program manager usually acts as more of a "center of excellence" and a coordinator, while project managers make more of the decisions about budgets and resources. Mediating resource disputes is more difficult in a decentralized model.

The role of the program manager varies significantly between ERP and e-business programs. An ERP is, by nature and design, an effort to integrate the enterprise more tightly. It focuses on the internal processes of the enterprise. It is more concise in its objectives and acts as a forcing function toward centralization of the enterprise, because it demands common process structures and a common view of data.

E-business, however, is outward looking and enables business strategies as opposed to business processes. In this more strategic atmosphere, the program manager has more responsibility for helping project managers to adhere to business decisions on how to deliver products and services to customers and how to communicate with business partners. These strategic business decisions—which must be developed, implemented, and monitored—have to do with the look and feel of a Web site, the way data is presented, and the way business transactions are performed. The look and feel of a Web site results in a market presence on the Web and contributes significantly to corporate branding. In essence, program managers delivering Web-based technology must consider themselves, to some extent, brand managers, and this requires a different approach than managing an ERP program.

PROJECT MANAGEMENT

Good project managers, whether they are working with an ERP installation or an e-business effort, possess five critical attributes:

1. They are intelligent and willing to learn.

2. They communicate well.

3. They are respected throughout the company or the business unit.

4. They are experienced in technology, change management, and business processes.

5. They are good cheerleaders.

Project managers are the external faces of the projects. They are the liaisons between the members of the various project teams and all those within the organization who are not involved with the project on a day-to-day basis, including senior leadership as well as employees at other levels.

Most ERP programs are structured hierarchies, with sets of projects reporting or monitored by central program offices and sets of activity-set or process teams reporting to project managers. E-business projects require coordination at a higher level and are often shorter, with more specific customer-related goals. Part of this coordination is due to the nature of the "new paradigm" e-business business model, but some of it is also that e-business projects are not usually as tightly intertwined with one another at a technical level but require coordination into a coherent program for overall success on the Web.

E-business managers and project teams within an enterprise that has successfully established an ERP backbone can spend less time coordinating projects and more time managing branding and successfully communicating and coordinating with business partners. Most e-business applications are delivered using standardized Web-browser interfaces, which should have an intuitive point-and-click feel. This means that training efforts can focus less on the how-to's of a system and more on business issues related to why and when.

However, e-business project managers do have to worry about a host of other issues that project managers in ERP installations do not have to worry about. These include most notably the need for a simple, intuitive look and feel as well as "help" to be designed into the

Figure 11-1   Project Success Is Based on Time, Cost, and Quality

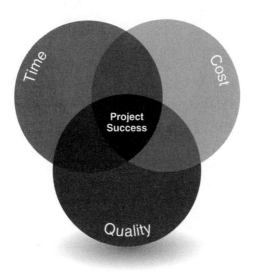

outside-facing Web pages; for the security of any transactions carried out using the Web; for coordination between the Web-based front-end technology and the back-office ERP or legacy systems; and for coordination of process, data, and communication between business partners. As with an ERP installation, project managers working on e-business implementations have to focus on the three key elements of project planning: targets, scope, and resources. Targets are usually shorter term in e-business efforts, with fewer intermediate milestones than in an ERP implementation. The scope is usually rather narrow and should be easy to define. The resources needed are usually easy to define, although not always easy to acquire since e-business is a "hot technology" and all companies are looking for people with the resources to get their e-business efforts up and running. In addition, as illustrated in Figure 11-1, any company involved in an ERP/e-business initiative must consider the impact of time, cost, and quality tradeoffs, and attempt to achieve an optimal balance among the three.

If a company is trying to implement Web-based technology and install or upgrade an ERP system at the same time (what we call trying to "stretch" in its migration), the overlay of the two different programs and project sets can cause some difficulties and must be closely coordinated. This can be extremely difficult, since the two efforts are often structured very differently and their natural rhythms are different.

12

ERP Vendor Responses to E-Business Challenges

E-business investments in the business-to-business market are already creating an increasingly interconnected and efficient web of business partners and demanding that ERP find a new purpose. ERP vendors are working hard to formulate and execute strategies to be a part of the e-business model. In the e-business world, a company must change its thinking about what ERP provides. Whereas in the early 1990s ERP was touted as an enabler of more streamlined business processes and a strategic investment that helped create world-class systems infrastructure, today ERP is considered the basic plumbing through which data moves to sophisticated decision-support and other tools that turn data into useful business information. Installing and maintaining ERP is tactical.

While throughout the 1990s a well-running ERP was considered an element of competitive advantage, that advantage really came from supply-chain management (SCM) and customer relationship management (CRM) systems. Yet, without ERP, neither SCM nor CRM works to its full potential. ERP vendors have seen their flanks attacked by niche-market technology providers who are building systems to perform the tasks of connecting one enterprise to another. Some are front-end buy or sell technologies; others are more sophisticated CRM or SCM systems. Some claim to be able to link to one another within an enterprise in such a way as to eliminate the need for an ERP system. To date, we do not believe these claims are credible. These "bolt-on" products are often difficult to integrate, requiring the use of intermediate or "middleware" products.

For the time being, there is no reason for a company that has installed an ERP system to rip it out; ERP is still the most useful and powerful transaction engine to move information within the enterprise. We believe that ERP will continue to be the transactional backbone on which decision support, data warehousing, and e-business applications connect. To maintain a position in the e-world, however, ERP vendors will need to embark on some combination of three strategic initiatives:

1. *Extend ERP functionality.* To support e-business, ERP systems of the future will not be what they were in the twentieth century. They will be designed and built on cross-enterprise interconnectivity that integrates across business partners using Internet protocol (IP) and include integrated sales and marketing and supply-chain management; customer relationship management; human resources; finance; and engineering and design. They will continue to provide increasingly sophisticated decision-support modeling, data-warehousing solutions, and CRM functionality.

2. *Build communities of users through portals and trading exchanges.* ERP vendors will seek to create trading communities, either by themselves or with partners, through Web portals that capitalize on their brand of ERP software. When put together, these strategies on the part of ERP vendors seek to both broaden the base of ERP customers—either managed in-house, outsourced to a service provider, or "rented" by an application service provider (ASP)—as well as to deepen the use of ERP functionality within customer companies.

170

3. *Create new ERP delivery models.* To help companies meet the high cost of ERP installation and maintenance, ERP vendors will increasingly seek to create models that allow companies to outsource dedicated ERP technology to outside service providers for system management. Existing ERP software companies and (potentially) some new entrants or partnerships of several companies will also provide a service, allowing customers to purchase ERP applications on a per-transaction or per-seat basis. This kind of service will rely heavily on the Internet as the delivery mechanism.

Figure 12-1 illustrates the difference between ERP and e-business applications in a number of dimensions.

EXTEND ERP FUNCTIONALITY

In the e-world, the focus is no longer just on how well an application can store and manage data and move it around within the enterprise. It is now on both adding value to that data to turn it into information and knowledge, and on moving that data and information across

Figure 12-1   ERP versus E-Business Applications

Dimensions	ERP Apps	E-Business Apps
Employees	Customers	Vendors
Focus	Inside Company Out	Outside Company In
Release Process	Periodic, Complex Upgrade	Continuous, Small Changes
Method of Integrating with Other Businesses	Through APIs or EDI	Browser, Portals, IT
Business Processes	Complex	Simple
User Interface	User Training Required	Intuitive

enterprises to create knowledgeable extended enterprises. Some areas in which ERP software packages will be expanded are:

- Customer relationship management
- Advanced planning and scheduling
- Value-based strategic management.

In a 1999 survey of 800 U.S. companies with from $30 million to $80 billion in revenues, AMR Research asked, What is the "first, most important selection criteria" for an ERP vendor? For 40 percent of companies, SCM is the most important. Another 17 percent said CRM; and another 15 percent said e-business. In contrast, fewer than 10 percent of respondents said industry experience is the most important criterion, and fewer than 5 percent said business intelligence is most important.

Customer Relationship Management

In the past, CRM technology was interfaced to a company's ERP; today, the applications are increasingly available over the Web and as part of an ERP suite. Web-based CRM applications include customer self-service; data mining used to define and capitalize on buying patterns; and data-driven personalization focused on selling based on customer-demonstrated preferences, as captured in their click patterns. But this data must reside somewhere; ERP applications tied to e-business applications and data warehouses are two options.

Customer delight is the key to enhancing revenue. Research has shown that only delighted customers are truly loyal. Customer delight provides a level of customer satisfaction that keeps customers coming back. Information technology (IT) allows nimble companies to strengthen their consumer relationships by integrating sales, product configuration, planning, and design processes with customers.

With CRM systems, a company can capture data about customers in hopes of identifying unique buying attributes or trends. However, not until the application of the Web have businesses operating in a mass-production world been truly able to personalize relationships with customers. In the world of e-business, companies have the opportunity to replicate the personal customer relationship that existed prior to mass markets. Companies are able to use knowledge of the customer to personalize customer service while continuing to sell standard products. CRM is the way to do this.

According to the GartnerGroup, "CRM is achieved by combining skilled customer-facing personnel, optimal processes, and enabling technologies, to balance optimal enterprise revenue and profits with maximum customer satisfaction." *Combining* is the keyword. To be effective, CRM must be seen as a combination of people, processes, and systems rather than as a narrowly defined IT application. CRM is one of the pieces of the new wave of ERP applications that focus on outward-facing processes, tying them together with the inside-the-enterprise transaction-processing engine of the original ERP systems. With ERP systems in place in many companies, the backbone exists on which to build CRM. CRM implies a "new marketing" that hinges on combining four key technologies: technology-enabled selling, call centers, e-business, and data warehousing and data mining to provide seamless customer service.

Advanced Planning and Scheduling

Globalization, along with shorter product life cycles and larger product variations, are combining to make it more important than ever for companies to maximize the effectiveness of their supply chains. While ERP systems have within them the ability to integrate information flows within supply-chain activities, ERP logic is based on the logic of manufacturing resource planning (MRP II). Advanced planning and scheduling (APS) software provides a better way of managing supply-chain activity information flows.

Although APS systems function like any other planning software, enabling 100 percent service delivery to customers while minimizing costs to the company, they distinguish themselves from ERP planning software by allowing managers to manipulate the supply chain in real time. The software provides value in three main areas:

1. Constraint-based planning
2. Real-time processing
3. Integration.

While materials requirement planning (MRP) and its successors MRP II and ERP deal with multiple constraints simply by providing the planner with exception reports, APS software weighs all of the constraints—materials, labor, machines, and warehousing and logistics—and suggests optimum planning scenarios to balance those constraints in order to provide the highest level of customer service at the lowest cost to the company. And while MRP-based planning tools consider one aspect of the supply chain at a time, such as materials or capacity, APS systems are modular and can be constructed to provide simultaneous consideration of multiple resource constraints. This, in turn, provides a truly integrated solution to the problems of supply-chain management.

Companies that have moved to APS software have seen improvements that include inventory reductions of between 20 and 70 percent, cost reductions of up to 12 percent, and reduced capital of up to 15 percent. More important, however, they have seen increased sales due to better customer service of between 2 and 15 percent, improved production throughput of 2 to 6 percent, and improved customer response at lower total cost. But quantifiable results are not the only benefits. APS is also a key enabler of process and behavioral changes. The production organization can move from being functionally based to being process driven. Planners can better leverage knowledge to make better decisions. And the production organization can adapt more quickly and effectively to changing customer requirements.

Value-Based Strategic Management

Corporate decisions fall into one of three categories: investment, financial, or operational. Investment or financial decisions are based on discounted cash flow (DCF) models or ROV™. When it comes to operational decisions, however, companies do not always make them with shareholder value in mind. To be certain that value creation can be sustained, managers at all levels need to make coherent, value-based decisions. To properly support value-based decision making, a company's information systems must include the following important attributes:

- Relevant information must be accessible at the point of decision making.
- The system must be flexible in order to reflect changes in organizational structures and processes and in the marketplace.
- It must be possible to view the data in dimensions that are relevant to the enterprise. For example, sales by country, sales by product line, profit by business unit, and lead-time by factory, to name just a few.
- The system must have multiuser access, which allows for a common source of information for decision makers across the organization.
- There must be consistency and integrity of data, and that data must be available in a timely manner so all users will have confidence in the information.
- The system must be user friendly for nonfinancial and non-IT decision makers.
- The system needs to be responsive, dynamic, and highly automated to support real-time decision making, and open to integration with third-party applications that improve functionality.
- Finally, it must be robust and have the ability to scale up to integrate large volumes of data from diverse sources.

In such an integrated system, data from both internal and external sources must be consolidated and compared with targets as part of the performance measurement process. This is the act of turning data into management information. This information is then transformed by simulation and scenario modeling into knowledge to form the base of strategic planning. Plans are translated into targets to drive the management of operational performance, and so the cycle is completed.

As well as consolidating historical performance, a company needs to be able to consolidate forward-looking information, including budgets, rolling forecasts, and latest estimates. To provide unbiased business intelligence and a sound basis for decision making, internal information must be considered in context with information from external sources. With the Internet, accessing external information is no longer a problem. The challenge is to find the salient facts among the vast quantity of data. Continuously changing, often unstructured, and typically qualitative rather than quantitative, external data is difficult to filter and assimilate.

In the past, without appropriate tools, many companies used external information in an informal, sporadic way. In the information age, the pace of change makes a more systematic approach essential. All of the major ERP vendors are working to provide some sort of value-based strategic management capability, from PeopleSoft's Enterprise Performance Management Workbench to modules by Oracle and SAP.

Shared Services

The ability to extend ERP functions onto the Web opens the way for a change in how shared service centers (SSCs) are organized. Utilizing Web-based technology, employees working at remote locations can conduct the work of shared services, creating a virtual SSC. The same Internet technology that allows customers to access order-fulfillment information and suppliers to access demand information creates opportunities for putting many human resource activities on a "self-service" model. Such "employee care" activities are becoming an increasingly large part of SSCs in an Internet-enabled world.

PORTALS, COMMUNITIES, AND TRADING EXCHANGES

The major benefits of Web-based buying and selling will be realized when production planning and procurement of all materials—production and nonproduction—are Web-enabled and integrated. To date, ERP vendors, vendors of specialty systems, companies in various industries, and dot.com companies are creating portals, communities, and trading exchanges of one kind or another. Some deal only with buying and selling at one stage of production, while others encompass direct materials, indirect materials, subcontractors, feeder plants, and transportation optimization.

Currently, portals, communities, and trading exchanges are emerging, and are not yet tightly linked with ERP. Some ERP vendors are trying to set up their own portals, while others are linking with partners to create either horizontal portals across a particular industry, or vertical portals that focus on a target industry segment. The big question about portals is whether industries will launch many, or only a few, and whether they will be open or proprietary. To date, many are proprietary, and the question is: How much can a proprietary portal grow before it hits its natural limit?

Portals and business communities are rapidly emerging business concepts, and the companies involved in developing them are quickly consolidating. For instance, in late December 1999, Ariba (a manufacturer of nonproduction procurement software and manager of nonproduction procurement catalogs for companies) agreed to buy Tradex Technologies (a creator of electronic marketplaces) for $1.86 billion in Ariba stock. VerticalNet, an early entrant into the independent trading exchange business, issued an initial public offering (IPO) in 1999 and used the proceeds to begin acquiring vertical trading exchanges. Some trading exchanges are allowing industry participants to take equity stakes as a means not only of raising cash, but also of validating the concept and the particular company's operations. DuPont has invested in CheMatch, and Dow has invested in ChemConnect.

NEW ERP DELIVERY MODELS

In the same way that ERP will not look the same in the future as it has in the past, it will, in many cases, also be delivered to customers in different ways. In the future, the hardware that runs an ERP system will not necessarily physically sit in the enterprise's facility or be managed by the enterprise. This role will be filled by ERP outsourcers and ASPs. Applications maintenance and services, business process, and data center management can all be outsourced.

In addition to traditional customers and ASPs, a new, nontraditional player has appeared on the ERP scene: Since 1996, BizTone has been developing an ERP system that can be delivered only via the Internet. The company, which set up shop in Asia in 1999, leases its ERP application, as well as other applications that can interface with its ERP, to clients around the world. While the traditional ERP vendors have retrofitted their ERP systems to work over the Web, BizTone developed its ERP software using a version of the Java language to deliver its basic system over the Web.

The value to a company in having a relationship with a traditional outsourcer, an ASP, or a provider of Internet-based services depends on the complexity of the application being utilized, on either a transactional, long-term lease, or owned-with-outside-maintenance basis. In any instance, clients are afforded the ability to have the most recent software upgrades, which are installed on the service provider's servers and appear in a transparent fashion to the user. The savings, in terms of installation, training, and ongoing maintenance, can be considerable.

WHERE THE PLAYERS ARE

Currently, ERP vendors are working to Web-enable their traditional modules; to add e-buy and e-sell modules; to integrate extended value chains; to provide customers with remote-hosted implementation options; and to develop portals, either alone or in combination with other application vendors or industry participants. All this is being done in an effort to beat back the niche players banging on the enterprise's doors from the outside. Figure 12-2 is an overview of e-business functionality and of software providers that are competing for that space.

SAP, with a 30 percent market share of installed ERP systems (12,000 customers), is working to Web-enable its current suite of modules. The company, which built its ERP modules around tightly defined business processes, is currently extending those processes into what it calls business scenarios that cross enterprise lines. SAP is also experimenting with providing outsourced operation of ERP modules, working with third parties that provide the capability to manage ERP on an outsourced basis.

In addition, the company has created mySAP.com, an on-line workplace through which it hopes to create 20 vertical trading exchanges, called marketplaces, within key industries in which the company has a large installed base, as well as to provide ASP services to companies that do not now use SAP technology. As of October 1999, the company had opened some of the marketplaces, but in most cases the big issues such as trading rules, policies and procedures, pricing, and data center management were not yet fully defined.

Oracle was the first of the big ERP vendors to begin Web-enabling its modules. The company is currently upgrading to add CRM technology to its suite. Oracle has also moved into the world of alternative delivery through Oracle's Business Online (BOL), through which the company sells ERP software and then manages it for a fee. According to Oracle, BOL makes the company the largest ASP in Europe and the Americas.

In September 1999, Oracle announced a joint venture with Ford Motor Company to be called AutoXchange. The goal of AutoX-change was to provide Ford and its vendor base a trading community through which it could purchase. Ford suppliers would be able to use the portal to purchase from each other, even when the purchases were not going into goods manufactured for Ford's end use. GM and Commerce One announced a similar venture in October 1999. However, suppliers pressured Ford, General Motors, and Daimler-

Figure 12-2 ERP Vendors' E-Business Capabilities

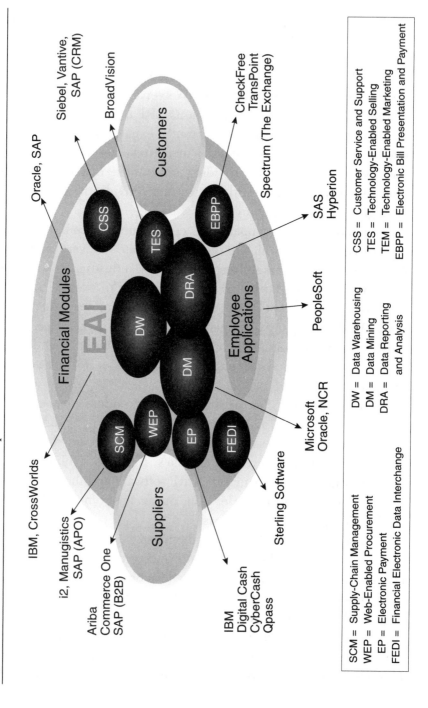

180

Chrysler—which had not yet created an Internet marketplace—to provide a common standard. The three automakers and two technology companies each have equity in the new venture. Other industries are following suit, for example, Sears, Oracle, and Carrefour of France in the retail industry.

PeopleSoft distributed an e-procurement package in the summer of 1999, and also purchased Vantive Corporation to acquire CRM technology. PeopleSoft has also developed a suite of strategic management analytical applications called *Enterprise Performance Management*. Beginning in early 2000, PeopleSoft joined with the retailer GUESS? and Commerce One to create a portal for apparel industry suppliers, manufacturers, and retailers. The system utilizes PeopleSoft eProcurement and Supply-Chain Management solutions, combined with Commerce One's MarketSite, that company's business-to-business portal technology.

PeopleSoft is also working with Gallaudet University, in Washington, D.C., the world's only liberal arts college for the deaf, to design a self-service e-business environment for students and faculty to gain access to the school's ERP information base. Students can use the systems to browse the catalog, check their grades, and add or drop courses; faculty can enter grades, check class rosters, and perform other administrative tasks.

J. D. Edwards is working to Web-enable its basic ERP suite under the name OneWorld, and get into the supply-chain management arena through its purchase of Numetrix. The company hopes that because its product has always separated business logic from the application and data, it will be more flexible and that customers will be able to attach e-business front-end technologies more easily. The company also created the ActivEra portal, through which users can gain access to both J. D. Edwards ERP suite and third-party software applications, such as Siebel Systems' CRM software.

Baan has built its e-business applications around Microsoft's site server commerce platform software; the suite includes three modules—E-Sales, E-Collaboration, and E-Procurement—each of which is a simple, relatively inexpensive self-service application.

The company i2 has traditionally been a supply-chain management software vendor, selling sophisticated APS software. But it is possible that the company, most likely in the near term, will break into the enterprise from the outside. The company manufactures SCM software that, according to the Atlanta-based research company Miller-Williams, has already saved customers billions of dollars through integration of supply chains, mostly in the computer manufacturing industry. i2 is also beginning to develop industry portals for its customers to link with each other. In late 1999, i2 launched its own portal called TradeMatrix which includes decision-support–optimizing embedded logic. A portal client can calculate constraints and lot size and perform APS and collaborative planning within the portal. It can then plug those calculations into its own decision-support system.

HOW WILL COMPANIES CONNECT?

To date, e-business is still an integrated modular architecture. No company has yet set the standard by which other companies will have to work. The question remains: How will companies connect? Will it be ERP to ERP; one company's buy-side to another company's sell-side; or through third-party integrators—either single-party or multiparty portals?

ERP vendors are all banking on portals to one extent or another. They see this strategy, as well as that of offering alternative models of providing ERP—through outsourcing or ASP relationships—as an opportunity to continue gaining either installed base or renters, and to continue their growth despite e-business. Outside analysts agree. AMR Research believes that ERP vendors will continue to grow at a rate of about 30 percent per year from 2000 through 2005, half their rate of growth from 1995 to 2000, but still healthy growth. It is not likely that they will all continue to grow. As we stated in our discussion of valuation models for ERP and e-business, at some point every company has to close off some of the options that e-business opens for it, pick a strategy, and execute that strategy effectively.

If companies want to connect with each other, to pass robust information back and forth and make their extra-enterprise relationships more efficient and effective, they will need to settle on a language, grammar, and syntax for data. Those software providers (traditional ERP vendors or others) that develop the most open systems, which make it easy for companies to work together, will be the winners. E-business requires tight collaboration among trading partners, but most ERP systems are not yet technically prepared to facilitate this. ERP was originally designed to function in an electronic data interchange (EDI)–enabled world; today, ERP vendors are at stages in transforming themselves for the Web-enabled world. This will require most client companies to rework, upgrade, extend, and in a few cases even replace or reimplement their existing ERP systems, which are fast becoming "legacy." The necessary level of collaboration, however, could not have been foreseen when most large, global corporations began their implementations in the mid-1990s.

No single application will provide or create competitive advantage. Currently, an integration of vendor-supplied ERP, decision-support tools, middleware, customer development, and Web sites among trading partner communities are all required to achieve the promised benefits of e-business. There is still an enormous amount of system integration that needs to go on in any large company seriously looking to become e-nabled. There is no silver bullet.

Glossary

Advanced Planning and Scheduling (APS)	A sophisticated set of decision-support applications that uses linear programming logic to identify optimal solutions to complex planning problems that are bound by material, labor, or capacity resource constraints.
Applet	A highly portable, machine-independent application component that can be executed either on a Web server or locally within a client browser. Applets are installed, maintained, and upgraded on the server, and are transparently downloaded on demand whenever they are needed. They are stored on the client machine and "refreshed" from the server the next time the client connects to that particular server.
Applications Programming Interface (API)	A set of calling conventions that define how a series is invoked through software. API allows programs written by users or third parties to communicate with certain vendor-supplied programs, which in turn allows users and third parties to add functions to vendor-supplied software.

Glossary

Applications Service Provider (ASP)	A company that provides software applications for "rent" over the Internet. Some ERP vendors are setting themselves up as ASPs, hoping to reach small and mid-sized companies that cannot afford the cost of licensing, installing, and operating ERP products that may be obsolete by the time they are fully installed and running. Other ERP companies are licensing their software to third-party ASPs, which own and operate software from many vendors. An ASP differs from an application outsourcer in that, while the outsourcer works on a one-to-one basis with each client, the ASP provides a "vanilla" solution.
Business Process Outsourcing	The provision of a noncore business processes, such as accounts payable, benefits management, or logistics, on a contracted basis.
Customer Relationship Management (CRM)	An integrated combination of software tools, business processes, and employee skills that allows a company to provide enhanced sales and service to customers, including personalized marketing, promotion, and even pricing.
Enterprise Resource Planning (ERP)	The information pipeline system within a company, which allows the company to move internal information efficiently so that it may be used for decision support inside the company and communicated via e-business technology to business partners throughout the value chain.
Extensible Markup Language (XML)	XML shares the same roots as Hypertext Markup Language (HTML), the language of the Internet. However, XML tags data so that it can be understood by any user on any computer platform.
Firewall	Dedicated hardware and software systems that provide security by screening network traffic and validating information flow between networks. A firewall protects a company's internal computing environment from infiltration.

Hypertext Markup Language (HTML)   The language used to create a hypertext document. Hypertext documents are commonly the underlying formatting for the World Wide Web. They provide a way to display documents on different browsers and machines.

Java   An object-oriented programming language developed by Sun Microsystems. JAVA can be used either to develop Internet applets, or as a general-purpose application development language. A Java program is written to run on a hypothetical computer known as the Java Virtual Machine (JVM). Any operating system or application that mimics a JVM can run a Java program.

Materials Requirement Planning (MRP)   The earliest manufacturing planning software, developed in the 1960s, it calculated which materials were required at what manufacturing operation and when they were required.

Manufacturing Resource Planning (MRP II)   An enhancement of MRP, adding a layer of sophistication to the basic calculations of MRP, but not changing the logic structure. MRP II was developed in the 1980s.

Portal   A portal window into an integrated set of Internet-based information or business tools. Portals can be established by a software vendor to Web-enable its suite of tools, by an industry participant to join together suppliers and purchasers throughout the value chain, or by a third party in an effort to aggregate and intermediate purchasing and selling, either within an industry or across industries by product.

Shared Services   The consolidation of noncore business processes from a company's business units into one organization. The shared service concept is based on service levels and mutual benefit to the business units and the shared service organization. Offloading noncore processes affords business unit leaders the opportunity to focus on their strategic activities.

Supply Chain Management (SCM)	The set of activities, tools, and software that allows a company to more tightly integrate production across business partners within a value chain. Supply-chain management software includes sophisticated planning software such as ASP.
Transmission Control Protocol/Internet Protocol (TC/IP)	A suite of protocols that defines the Internet and allows communication between different types of computers and networks connected to the Internet.
Web Browser	Software that allows a user to view and interact with content on the World Wide Web or on a company's intranet or extranet. The browser processes text, graphics, and in some cases sound and video. It also downloads and processes files as required. The browser's most basic responsibilities are making a request for data to a server, interpreting the data it receives, and presenting the data to the user.
Web Server	The combination of hardware and software that retrieves Internet Web information and transfers Web pages to a Web browser. The Web server also provides messaging, data, interaction management, and secure communications.
Web Server Application Programming Interface (API)	Addresses interaction between the Web servers and corporate data and enables information to flow between the browser, Web server, and corporate data store. For example, the API allows authorized users to use a browser to view financial reports generated directly from the back-office accounting system database.

Index

Index

Customer Benefit Limited, Reduced
E-Options and Flexibilty, ERP/
e-business matrix, 139–140
Customer demand, 34
Customer relationship management (CRM):
call centers, 101–102
data mining, 104–105
data warehousing, 104–105
defined, 6, 23, 35
development of, 97–98, 169–170
e-nabled call centers, 102
field service, 103–104
internet protocol (IP) telephony, 103
need for, 98–99
technology-enabled selling (TES), 99–101
vendor response and, 172–173
Customer-supplier relationship, 36, 173
Customer-value drivers, 46

DaimlerChrysler, 181
Data integrity, 93, 146
Data mining, customer relationship
management (CRM), 104–105
Data standards, 146
Data warehousing, 71, 104–105
Decentralization, 73, 77
Decision-making:
organizational, 53
systems, 52–53
value-based, 174–175
Decision-support technology, 43, 175
Delivery models, 171, 178
Dell Computer, 94, 101
Demand chain management, 30–31, 69
Deployment, in implementation process, 52
Discounted cash flow (DCF) analysis:
application of, generally, 151, 175
characteristics of, 48–49
ROV™ analyis distinguished from, 53, 58, 61–63
Disruptive technologies:
characteristics of, 9–12
valuation, 47
Dot.com companies, 6, 58–59, 140
Dow, 177
Dream Tree™, 61
DuPont, 177

eBay, 95
E-business, generally:
assumptions, 16
change capability, 129
change complexity, 129

change-management approach, 130–136
cultural challenge, 130
customer focus, 35–36
defined, 14–16
ERP, relationship with, 1–4
focus of, 27
historical perspective, 3–4
matrix, *see* E-business matrix
operational issues, 126–128
organizational scope, 128–129
political resistance, 129–130
sponsorship, executive, 125–126
value-chain partners, interactive relationships with, 36–40
E-business matrix:
defined, 17–18
options, 18–21
e-catalogs, 95
e-commerce, defined, 14–15
e-customer relationship management (eCRM), 19
800.com, 35
Electronic data interchange (EDI),
applications of, 14, 38, 42, 93, 142, 152, 183
e-logistics, e-supply chain management (e-SCM), 87–88
Emergency orders, 91
e-nabled call centers, customer relationship management (CRM), 102
e-nabling technology, 41–42
End-stage architecture, 42–44
End-to-end process, 76–77, 79, 123
Enterprise Growth Limited, ERP/e-business matrix, 139
Enterprise Performance Management Workbench, 176
Enterprise resource planning (ERP), generally:
assumptions, 16
customer demands and, 34
defined, 12–14
e-business, relationship with, *see* ERP/ E-business
focus of, 26
functionality of, 29
implementation of, *see* Implementation, of ERP
as internal technological hub, 25–26, 30–33
options, 6–7, 21–22
perception of, 4–6
e-partnering, 16
e-procurement:
e-supply chain management (e-SCM), 86
shared service centers (SSCs), 108–109

190

Index

Index

Index